THE COSTLY U.S. PRISON SYSTEM:

TOO COSTLY IN DOLLARS, NATIONAL PRESTIGE AND LIVES

by Paul Brakke

Author of: *American Justice?,*

The Price of Justice in America,

Cops Aren't Such Bad Guys,

Fixing the U.S. Criminal Justice System

and

The Great National Divides

THE COSTLY U.S. PRISON SYSTEM: TOO COSTLY IN DOLLARS, NATIONAL PRESTIGE AND LIVES

ACKNOWLEDGMENTS

I am indebted to Gini Graham Scott for much help in the preparation of this book. Further, I would like to acknowledge the assistance of publicist Jana Collins. Finally, I have received valuable insights on life in prison from several who spent time in prison or their relatives since I have no first-hand knowledge of prison. They wish to remain anonymous.

TABLE OF CONTENTS

PREFACE

More prisons may be the worst investment this country can make. Former Supreme Court Justices Stephen Breyer and Anthony Kennedy denounced the criminal justice system to a Congressional subcommittee in 2015, noting that it costs approximately $30,000 a year to incarcerate a prisoner in California, compared to $3500 a year for education of schoolchildren. Now multiply that by the number of prison inmates - 2.3 million. The tab is enormous -- well over $60 billion. That's $600 per U.S. household each year! And that figure is a gross underestimate if you consider the costs to the incarcerated, their families and communities, resulting in a final cost estimate of $1 trillion.[1]

Should we be trying harder to rehabilitate these people, so they can become productive, contributing members of society? Or do we really want to provide them free room and board behind bars at our expense?

It's certainly true that we have to lock up the worst in our society to keep them from harming us. But we have been doing too much of that, and too many of these criminals aren't the worst in our society. We've run out of prison space. We put offenders on probation because we can't afford to lock up any more. We're constantly constructing new prisons, and the prisoners we release keep on offending, winding back up in the slammer as recidivists (repeat offenders) in no time.

---

[1] Michael McLaughlin, Carrie Pettus-Davis, Derek Brown, Chris Veeh and Tanya Renn, "The Economic Burden of Incarceration in the U.S.", Working Paper #CI072016, Concordance Institute for Advancing Social Justice, George Warren Brown School of Social Work, Washington University in St. Louis, July, 2016.

Former NYPD Commissioner, life-long law-and-order Republican Bernard Kerik, laments about the "insane money our country wastes on incarcerating people who could be dealt with, punished in alternative ways."[2]

A badly needed 2015 bipartisan Sentencing Reform and Corrections Act failed to pass, and it is doubtful whether President Trump and Attorney General Sessions will support any such efforts now.

Incarcerations must decrease. The high recidivism rate has to be lowered. This book will focus on ways to improve the prison and correctional systems, reduce the number of prison inmates, and prepare them for successful re-entry back into society.

[2]Bernard B. Kerik, *From Jailer to Jailed: My Journey from Correction and Police Commissioner to Inmate #84888-054*, Threshold Editions, 2015, p.126.

Currently those with the power to change the system are conservative suburbanites who have the least to do with the system, and therefore are the most ignorant of its faults. This book represents an attempt to remedy that situation.

By way of introduction, I am a biomedical scientist and concerned citizen, not a professional criminologist. But in the past three years, I have done extensive research on this subject, so I guess that makes me a newly minted expert. Many books have been written recently on the subject of crime and incarceration, and I have read a lot on the subject. Most of what I have read was written by liberals and for a professional criminologist audience, so it is lengthier and full of jargon that is likely to be inscrutable to a more general audience. I hope that this book will help fill that void by summarizing and analyzing conclusions drawn in those books and providing additional insight. I fear that not enough of the public, in particular the conservative public, is aware of the seriousness of the present situation, which calls for quick corrective action, lest we end up with unnecessarily high costs and mounting crime.

I am concerned that politicians of both stripes have allowed the system to evolve into the monstrosity it has become. Reform has to happen locally in the form of hundreds of grass roots movements, because so few of the incarcerated are under federal jurisdiction. This reform will be easiest to accomplish in states under one-party control, particularly in Republican-controlled states in the South and Midwest. In other parts of the country, it may take alliances between concerned citizens on the right (corporate and faith-based organizations) and the left (equal justice and civil rights advocates) to work together to fix the system.

INTRODUCTION

Though most U.S. citizens are probably unaware of this, the U.S. leads the world in incarcerations.[3]

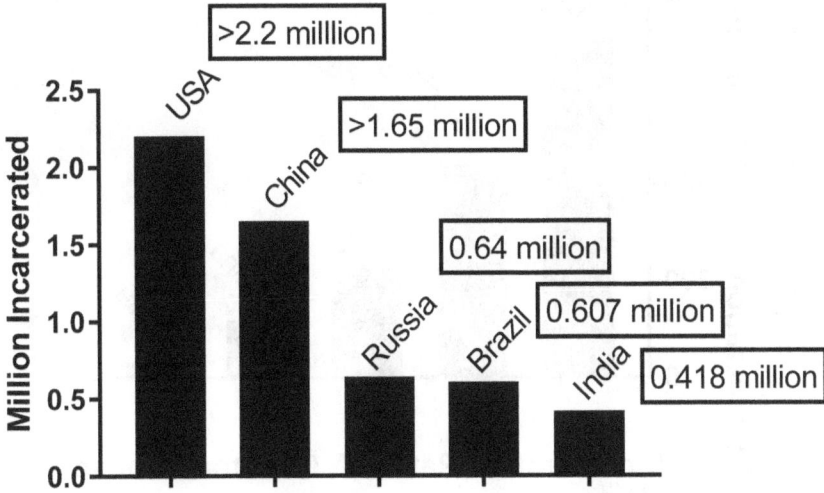

Top 5 Countries for Incarceration

Some of these statistics on other countries may be underestimated because of the way the prison population is recorded. For example, China detains another 650,000 individuals without sentencing them, which may correspond to part of the U.S. jail population. But China has a much

---

[3] Roy Walmsley, "World Prison Population List", 11th edition, World Prison Brief, Institute for Criminal Policy Research, Birkbeck University of London, 2016, http://www.prisonstudies.org/sites/default/files/resources/downloads/world_prison_population_list_11th_edition_0.pdf

larger population. If you normalize (divide) by the
population for each country, the U.S. still tops the list.[3]

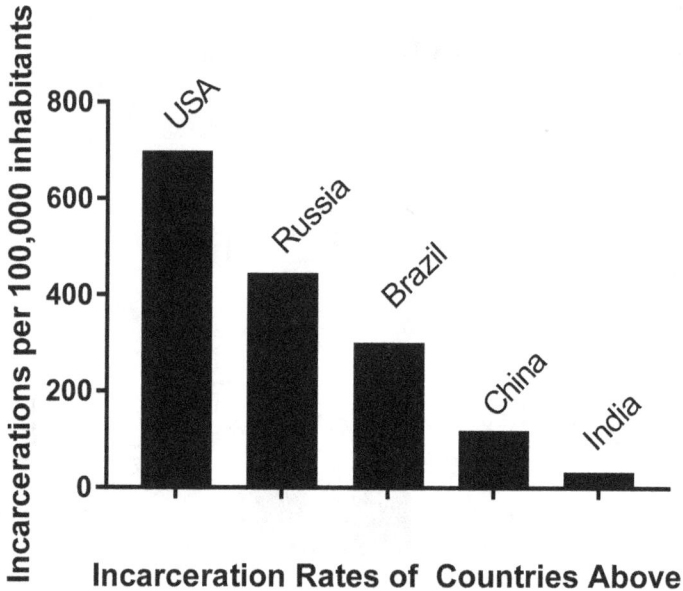

Incarceration Rates of Countries Above

For a country that prides itself on its human rights
record and seriously criticizes countries like Russia and China
for their poor treatment of people, we should examine
ourselves closely to make sure we are not guilty of hypocrisy.
We could be accused of having our own gulag, given our
horrendous incarceration record.

Why Do We Have So Many Prisoners?

Do we have so many more prisoners because we are a
much more violent nation than others? This isn't the case.

14

To illustrate, the chart below indicates that Russia and Brazil have a much higher murder rate than we do.[4]

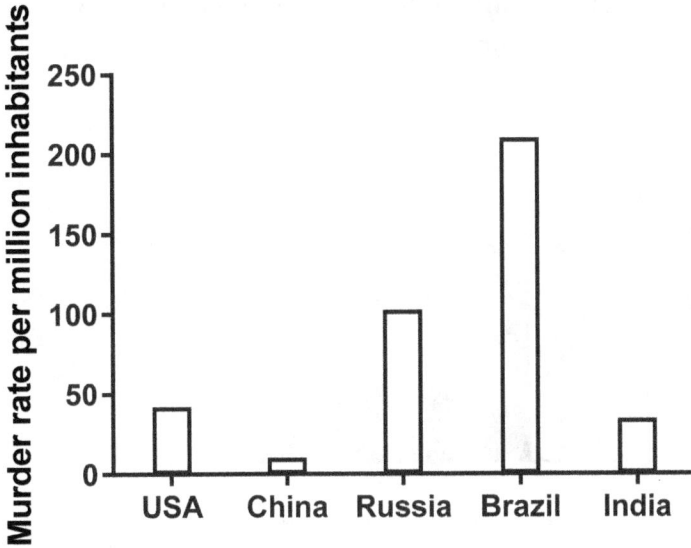

Therefore, there is no real excuse for the vast number of prisoners we have incarcerated. We have imprisoned so many millions in response to a crime wave that began in the 1960s. That may have helped reduce crime levels, but we still haven't fixed the crime problem sufficiently, and we have now added the additional problem that incarceration compounds the social ill that plagues our cities. That's because this extensive incarceration has further eroded the social structure of impoverished urban black communities, and this will continue to foster crime for decades to come

---

[4] NationMaster, "Crime>Violent Crime>Murder Rate per Million People: Countries Compared"; http://www.nationmaster.com/country-info/stats/Crime/Violent-crime/Murder-rate-per-million-people

unless we treat the condition that leads to criminal behavior --
much of it the result of poverty in the inner cities.

While some smaller countries approach the U.S. rate
of incarceration, no country of over a million inhabitants
does.[3]

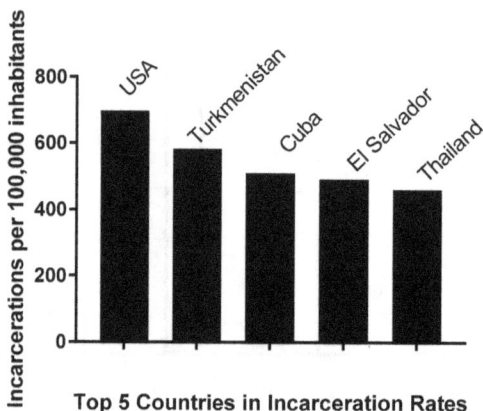

Top 5 Countries in Incarceration Rates

Thus, despite having lower incarceration rates, most of
these countries have similar murder rates as us, with the
exception of El Salvador, which exhibits one of the highest
murder rates of any country.[4] So proportionately, we are
putting more of our criminals in prison, even for nonviolent
crimes, than other countries. And ironically, many of these
are third-world less developed countries that have a higher
low-income and impoverished population compared to us.

Murder rate per million inhabitants

800 —
600 —
400 —
200 —
0 —

USA   Turkmenistan   Cuba   El Salvador   Thailand

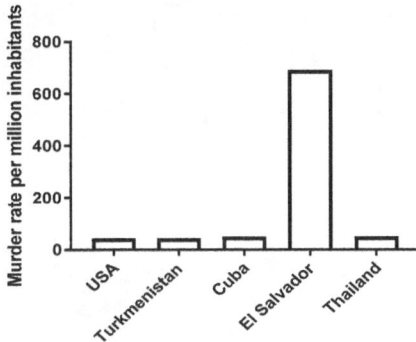

Ironically, we Americans pride ourselves on being first in many things, but incarceration should not be one of those. We experience similar levels of crime as European countries, but more violent crime,[5] and victims are more likely die in the U.S. It is likely that the fear of violent crime has led us to demand tougher punishment.[6] The result is on average about a six times higher incarceration rate than Europe has.

---

[5] Violent crime is defined as homicide, rape, assault and robbery.
[6] John F. Pfaff, *Locked In, The True Causes of Mass Incarceration and How to Achieve Real Reform*, Basic Books, 2017, p. 177

CHAPTER 1 – HOW DID WE GET HERE?

Recent History of Incarceration in the U.S.

As indicated on the graph below,[7] the greater than 5-fold rise in incarceration began in state prisons in the 1970s and continued until about 2008 through both three Republican and two Democratic Presidencies. Many people are also held in local jails, sometimes for months or even years before their trial or sentencing.

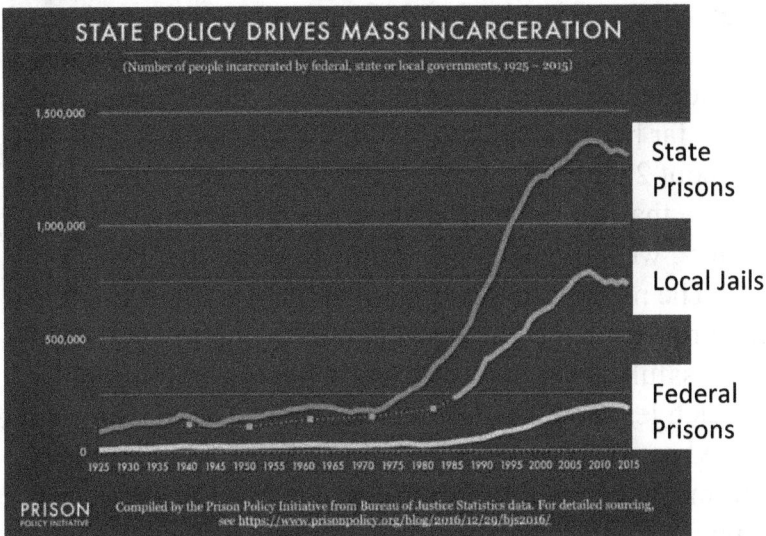

STATE POLICY DRIVES MASS INCARCERATION

(Number of people incarcerated by federal, state or local governments, 1925 – 2015)

State Prisons

Local Jails

Federal Prisons

PRISON POLICY INITIATIVE

Compiled by the Prison Policy Initiative from Bureau of Justice Statistics data. For detailed sourcing, see https://www.prisonpolicy.org/blog/2016/12/29/bjs2016/

After 2008, incarceration plateaued at all levels -- local, state, and federal, and even showed signs of a slight decrease.

---

[7] Graph: Courtesy of Prison Policy Initiative, 2017

Causes for the Rise in Incarceration

The best book I have read on the history of this subject is Elizabeth Hinton's *From the War on Poverty to the War on Crime: The Making of Mass Incarceration in America.*[8] Hinton details how successive administrations from John F. Kennedy on to George H. W. Bush recognized the problem of crime in urban black ghettos, but they were unable to stop its growth with either liberal or conservative tactics.

Both liberal and conservative administrations increased incarceration in response to concern among whites that crime would spread to their communities. The great riots in Watts in Los Angeles in 1965 and in Newark and Detroit in 1967 changed that concern about crime to real fear, and law and order became the cry among politicians of both stripes. Even as far back as the late 1970s, FBI data suggested that only about 250,000 criminals pursue careers in street crime.[9] Yet, now that we're incarcerating nearly ten times that many prisoners, we still have more crime than we did then.

The many alternate liberal strategies to solving the crime problem have not worked, after being tried unsuccessfully over 50 years ago, when the crime problem was much less acute than it has become. These efforts have included more community policing, police urban outreach programs, attempts to improve the conditions and security in substandard public housing projects, and increased job training. But none of these approaches have worked, primarily because of insufficient job opportunities for black

---

[8] Elizabeth Hinton, *From the War on Poverty to the War on Crime: The Making of Mass Incarceration in America*, Harvard University Press, 2016.
[9] Ibid, Chapter 7.

ghetto dwellers.[10] Greater incarceration became the only alternative.[11] As Richard Nixon explained in his call for a crackdown in crime in 1968: "Doubling the conviction rate in this country would do more to cure crime in America than quadrupling the funds for ... war on poverty."[12]

One result of this strategy was a massive drop in the income level of black households, as a result of the increasingly vast number of African-American males being carted off to prison for longer and longer terms. Or to put this conclusion more starkly in numbers, by 2000 the net financial assets of the top fifth of all black households ($7448) was only $448 higher than the lowest fifth of white households.[13]

Greater incarceration reflected the growing public attitude towards what Peter Enns called "public punitiveness." He came to this conclusion after conducting a more detailed analysis of the causes of the increased incarceration. To conduct his study, Peter Enns assessed public opinion about crime after World War II in response to various surveys that he condensed into a factor he termed public punitiveness.[14] Using correlation analysis similar to

---

[10] Elizabeth Hinton, *From the War on Poverty to the War on Crime: The Making of Mass Incarceration in America*, Harvard University Press, 2016, Chapters 2-3.
[11] Ibid, Chapters 4-9.
[12] James Kilgore, *Understanding Mass Incarceration: A People's Guide to the Key Civil Rights Struggle of Our Time*, The New Press, 2015, p. 18.
[13] Elizabeth Hinton, *From the War on Poverty to the War on Crime: The Making of Mass Incarceration in America*, Harvard University Press, 2016, Epilogue.
[14] Peter K. Enns, *Incarceration Nation: How the United States Became the Most Punitive Democracy in the World*, Cambridge University Press, 2016.

what I use later in this book, he argued convincingly that the root cause of the increase in incarceration was this public punitiveness driven by the media, whereby the public demanded more law and order. This demand drove politicians of all stripes to enact the policies that resulted in increased incarceration.

This demand for punitiveness was a key factor because rising crime in the 1970s and 80s only explained about half of the rise in incarceration. That's because incarceration continued to increase in the 1990s and onward, even though violent crime began decreasing.[15]

To a great extent this growth of incarceration was due to a response to an urban crime wave in the 1960s, but then that led to an overreaction that has simply upped costs. This response to a crime wave is well documented in Barry Latzer's book *The Rise and Fall of Violent Crime in America.*[16] Latzer suggests that the migration of blacks from

---

[15] John F. Pfaff, *Locked In, The True Causes of Mass Incarceration and How to Achieve Real Reform*, Basic Books, 2017, p. 4.
[16] Barry Latzer, *The Rise and Fall of Violent Crime in America*, Encounter Books, 2015.

the rural South to northern cities after World War II was the key factor initially, since the homicide rate of blacks at the time was 10 times that of whites. As a consequence, a new wave of violent crime began in the 1960s in the larger cities, where most of the victims as well as most of the perpetrators were black.

In addition to the black urban migration, Latzer suggests that more baby boomers reaching adolescence contributed to the crime wave, because they overwhelmed the resources of the criminal justice system.[17] The response of the system was to increase incarceration. According to Latzer, the crime wave abated in the 1990s as a result of a combination of more police, more effective policing, increased commitments to prison, and increases in time served for violent crimes.

An Analysis of Violent Crime and Incarceration Statistics Since 1960

I have analyzed violent crime and incarceration statistics since 1960. These data[18] provide clear evidence of the following:

---

[17] Peak criminal activity occurs around age 20.

[18] "Uniform Crime Reporting Statistics, estimated violent crime rate", U.S. Department of Justice, https://www.ucrdatatool.gov/Search/Crime/State/RunCrimeTrendsinOne Var.cfm ; U.S. Department of Justice, Bureau of Justice Statistics Bulletin "Prisoners 1925-81", https://www.bjs.gov/content/pub/pdf/p2581.pdf; "Prisoners in Custody of State or Federal Correctional Authorities 1977-98", http://www.bjs.gov/index.cfm?ty=pbdetail&lid=2080 ; "Prisoners in 2000", http://www.bjs.gov/index.cfm?ty=pbdetail&lid=927; "Prisoners in 2005", http://www.bjs.gov/index.cfm?ty=pbdetail&lid=912;

❖ The rise in violent crime preceded and drove the initial rise in incarceration up until 1992;

❖ Incarceration continued to rise after 1992, finally causing violent crime to fall;

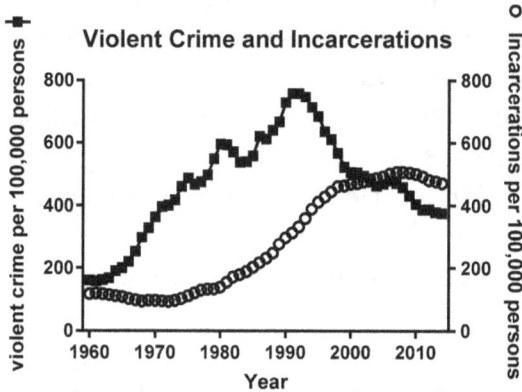

Violent Crime and Incarcerations

Note that violent crime rates peaked in 1992 and then declined. However, incarceration rates continued to rise until 2007. Thus, there was an approximately 15-year period when crime was falling and incarceration rising. After 2002 incarcerations actually surpassed violent crime. What should be concluded from these data?

First, over the period 1974 to 1992, when violent crime and incarceration were both increasing, incarceration rates were driven by violent crime rates, as revealed by the positive correlation below:[19,20,21]

"Prisoners in 2015", http://www.bjs.gov/index.cfm?ty=pbdetail&lid=5869

[19] In *The Price of Justice in America*, I used the same kind of correlation analysis to determine that guns were not a primary determinant of violent crime rates, but the proportion of poor blacks in a population was.

[20] See Appendix I for a short primer on correlation analysis. An r value of 0.7 or greater is considered a strong correlation, one greater than 0.5 a

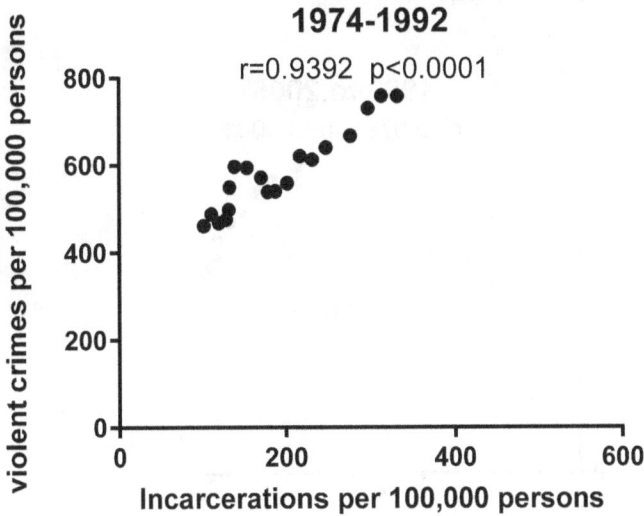

1974-1992

r=0.9392 p<0.0001

(y-axis: violent crimes per 100,000 persons; x-axis: Incarcerations per 100,000 persons)

There are two questions to be asked:

1) Does more violent crime lead to more incarcerations? The strong correlation indicates that it could. An alternative conclusion, that increased incarceration leads to increased violent crime, only makes sense if incarceration provides a school for criminals. Both are possible.

2) Does more incarceration lead to less violent crime? If this were true, a negative correlation would be found (dots should go down to the right rather than up), but this was not found.

More to the point, the relationship changed dramatically over the next twelve years. From 1993 to 2005,

---

moderate one, and one greater than 0.3 a weak one. A p value less than 0.05 is considered significant. This 1974-1992 correlation is extremely strong.

[21] There are only about half as many total incarcerations as there are violent crimes, since not all crimes are solved.

the correlation indicates that increased incarceration caused a decrease in violent crime:[22]

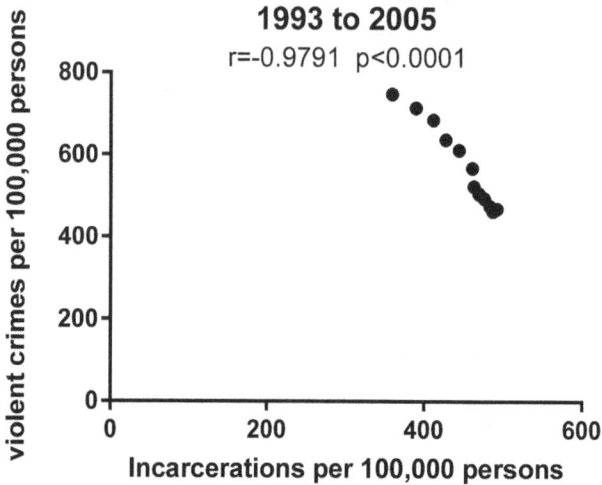

This conclusion is inescapable. The alternative conclusion that decreased violent crime causes increased incarceration defies credulity.

Finally, since 2006, the correlation became positive once again, but this time both crime and incarcerations were declining, suggesting that a decrease in violent crime is driving the decrease in incarcerations:

---

[22] This is one of the single strongest correlations that I have plotted among hundreds of such tests. It was totally unexpected and literally bowled me over when I encountered it.

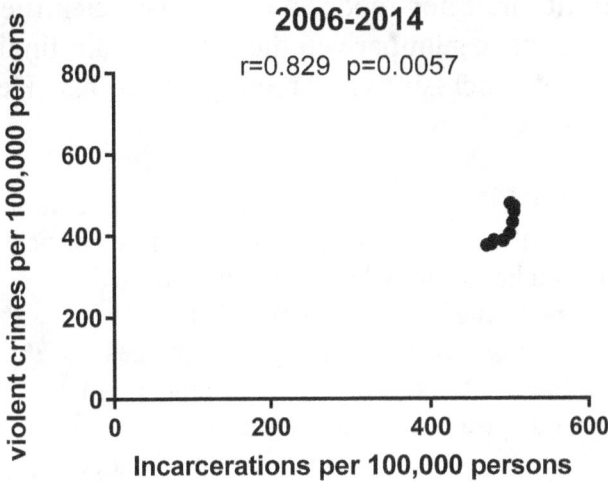

2006-2014

r=0.829 p=0.0057

y-axis: violent crimes per 100,000 persons
x-axis: Incarcerations per 100,000 persons

From this I conclude that increased incarceration may have led to a reduction of violent crime in the recent past, but that since 2006 it has not.[23] Analyses of other researchers are reviewed in Appendix II.

What Mechanisms Were Used to Increase Incarceration?

The rise in incarceration was managed by increasing sentence lengths and locking up more people for minor crimes and drug crimes, according to a 400+ page book published by the National Academies of Science in 2014.[24] This exhaustive tome summarizes two years of work by a 24-member committee and documents many studies. Though

---

[23] This is similar to conclusions by Pfaff in *Locked In*, but with a greater than ten-year delay in onset.
[24] Jeremy Travis, Bruce Western and Steve Redburn, Editors, *The Growth of Incarceration in the United States: Exploring Causes and Consequences*, National Academies Press, 2014.

these study results are often reported in abstruse scientific lingo, the authors have summarized the study's main findings in a short series of conclusions and recommendations. Here's its main conclusion:

"CONCLUSION: The unprecedented rise in incarceration rates can be attributed to an increasingly punitive political climate surrounding criminal justice policy formed in a period of rising crime and rapid social change. This provided the context for a series of policy choices —across all branches and levels of government—that significantly increased sentence lengths, required prison time for minor offenses, and intensified punishment for drug crimes."[25]

These same observations were echoed in a report by the liberal Brennan Center[26] which concluded that the increase in incarceration was primarily affected by the following factors:

❖ harsher sentencing laws, including mandatory minimum sentencing for many crimes;

❖ three-strikes and you're out laws, whereby even a minor third felony conviction resulted in an extremely long sentence;

[25] Jeremy Travis, Bruce Western and Steve Redburn, Editors, *The Growth of Incarceration in the United States: Exploring Causes and Consequences*, National Academies Press, 2014, p. 9.
[26] James Austin, Lauren-Brooke Eisen with James Cullen and Jonathan Frank, "How Many Americans are Unnecessarily Incarcerated?", Brennan Center for Justice, Twenty Years, 2016; https://www.brennancenter.org/sites/default/files/publications/Unnecessarily_Incarcerated.pdf

❖ harsh sentencing for non-violent drug possession or dealing of even small amounts of drugs.

However, while these are recognized as contributing causes, an even greater role was and still is played by prosecutors, accord to John Pfaff's 2017 book *Locked In*. As Pfaff points out, prison admissions per prosecutor rose from 9 in 1974 to 25 in 1990 and essentially stayed at similar levels since then.[27] This increase occurred when violent crime and incarcerations were both rising. What about when violent crime was dropping off but incarcerations continued to rise? Between 1994 and 2008, while crimes fell as well as arrests in most categories, the number of prosecutions rose, as would be expected if prosecutors contributed to the fall in crime. In addition, the rate at which prosecutors filed felony charges rose almost 40%, while the likelihood of this resulting in a prison stay remained the same;[28] thus resulting in nearly 40% more incarcerations and associated costs.

Prosecutors are able to exert so much influence, because they have a great deal of power. Unfortunately, they often abuse that power, certainly in Arkansas.[29] In fact, one of the prosecutors mentioned in that article used unscrupulous methods against my wife a number of years ago.[30]

To a lesser extent, wrong imprisonment of innocent individuals also contributes to high incarceration rates and

[27] John F. Pfaff, *Locked In, The True Causes of Mass Incarceration and How to Achieve Real Reform,* Basic Books, 2017, pp. 129-130.
[28] Ibid., pp 71-72.
[29] Mara Leveritt, "Prosecutors have all the power*", Arkansas Times,* September 11, 2014, paper front cover: "Weighted Justice. Powerful Prosecutors Go Unpunished".
[30] Paul Brakke, *American Justice?,* Touchpoint Press, 2016

costs, as well as unfairly imprisoning individuals who have committed no crime. This is a point made by Arkansas columnist Dana Kelley who described a 2013 survey sponsored by the Center for Prosecutor Integrity which found that 67% of respondents believed that the principle of "innocent until proven guilty" was being lost in our legal system. This survey also found that many states offer no compensation to those wrongly incarcerated, so that these innocent victims of the criminal justice system not only lose years of their lives in prison, but they lose thousands if not millions in lost income along with those disrupted lives.[31] Many lose their families as well as the potential for future income at the level they could have obtained had they not been incarcerated.

An even more scathing indictment of prosecutors may be found in former NYPD[32] Commissioner Bernard Kerik's book *From Jailer to Jailed*,[33] in which he pointedly argues against the current system of prosecutorial immunity. In his view, prosecutors should be criminally liable if they commit the crime of knowingly prosecuting a person they believe is innocent or withholding exculpatory[34] evidence from the defense. As examples, prosecutors were responsible for Michael Morton's conviction and 25-year prison stay for allegedly murdering his wife,[35] and they played a role in the false confession, conviction and a 12-year prison stay of Ron

---

[31] Dana D. Kelley, "Righting awful wrongs", *Arkansas Democrat-Gazette*, 6/2/2017.

[32] New York Police Department

[33] Bernard B. Kerik, *From Jailer to Jailed: My Journey from Correction and Police Commissioner to Inmate #84888-054*, Threshold Editions, 2015.

[34] Evidence that would exonerate the defendant.

[35] Michael Morton, *Getting Life: An Innocent Man's 25-Year Journey from Prison to Peace*, Simon & Schuster, 2015.

Williamson for murder,[36] before each was exonerated by DNA evidence. Similarly, Noura Jackson spent 9 years in prison for murder because prosecutors withheld evidence from her defense team, until that was exposed on appeal.[37]

Arguments from several books written by liberal authors are summarized briefly in Appendix II. I believe they are correct in some of their conclusions, but quite incorrect in others.

Misrepresenting the Extent of the Violent Crime Problem

Unfortunately, misrepresentations about the extent of recent violent crime and its cause abound. Here in Arkansas, columnist Dana D. Kelley has disputed incorrect assertions by the liberal media that crime is at historic lows to claim that violent crime rates are actually much higher now. To make his case, he cited violent crime rates of 383.2 in 2015 compared to only 160.9 in 1960.[38] While he is right that 383.2 is not a historic low, Mr. Kelley failed to point out that violent crime peaked at 758 in 1991, and thus crime rates have in fact decreased.[39]

---

[36] Dana D. Kelley, "On wrongful convictions", *Arkansas Democrat-Gazette*, 5/26/2017; John Grisham, *The Innocent Man,* (non-fiction), Penguin/Random House, 2008.

[37] Emily Bazelon, "Guilt by Omission", *NY Times* 8/6/2017.

[38] "Crime Wake-up Call," *Arkansas Democrat-Gazette* December 9, 2016.

[39] "Unnecessarily Incarcerated," Brennan Center, https://www.brennancenter.org/sites/default/files/publications/Unnecessarily_Incarcerated.pdf

Summing Up

This analysis has led to the following conclusions:

❖ Media coverage of anarchy starting in the 1960s stoked public fears about violent crime and fueled a demand for law and order.

❖ Politicians from both parties were fearful of seeming too soft on crime, so they pushed through punitive measures designed to lock up as many criminals as possible.

❖ Violent crime has diminished since its peak in the 1990s.

❖ Incarceration may have helped reduce violent crime in the 1990s, but it has not further reduced crime for at least 15 years.

CHAPTER 2 – FACTS ABOUT OUR PRISONS AND CORRECTIONAL SYSTEM

The Cost of Prisons

Today, the cost of prisons and the rest of our correctional system are out of control. We are spending far more than we need to, and we are getting poor results. Let me explain.

We spend $260 billion annually on criminal justice, $60-70 billion on prisons and jails alone. Most prisons are run by the states, not by the federal government. If all of them were federal prisons, the $60 billion it takes to run them would seem relatively modest in comparison to the defense budget, Social Security and Medicare. The costs to individual states and localities are significantly higher in proportion to their budgets, since states spend up to 3% of their budgets on prisons and counties spend roughly 2% of their budgets for jails.[40] However, many politicians are less concerned by the high cost of incarcerating people than they are by the great public concern about crime. Public concern has been fanned by the media since the 1960s and is an even greater concern to politicians anxious to be re-elected than is fiscal prudence.

These criminal justice costs not only include the most obvious payments for prisons and jails, but the hidden costs of the system, which result from:

❖ the cost of investigating the crime and trying or pleading the case,

---

[40] Pfaff, *Locked In*, 2017, pp. 12, 97.

❖ the cost to the economy due to the loss of the cost of living spending that could have been made by the convict if he had not been incarcerated,

❖ the consequent loss of tax revenue due to the imprisoned convict's lack of work,

❖ the consequent collateral costs to the ex-convict due to limiting his opportunity to support himself, and

❖ the consequent collateral costs to the family, particularly to the children and the mother of the convict's children, relegating them to a life of poverty, most often on welfare, paid by the taxpayer.

These costs and others more specific to white collar crime can raise the total cost to several times that of incarceration alone, as laid out forcefully by Bernard Kerik,[41] who suggests in one hypothetical example that these total amounts can be over 20 times the cost of incarceration alone. Thus, aside from making the traditional liberal arguments to support being more sympathetic to prisoners, even the liberal press has recognized the economic arguments for reducing unnecessary incarcerations. For example, the *Huffington Post* reported an estimate of the cost at over a trillion dollars annually, about half of which is due to lost income on the part of the incarcerated, their families and their communities.[42]

---

[41] Kerik, *From Jailer to Jailed*, pp. 265-6.
[42] Carrie Pettus-Davis, Washington Univ. St. Louis, referred to by Matt Ferner,"The Full Cost Of Incarceration In The U.S. Is Over $1 Trillion, Study Finds" *Huffington Post;*
http://www.huffingtonpost.com/entry/mass-incarceration-cost_us_57d82d99e4b09d7a687fde21

The Prison System

While liberals tend to make a big stink about private prisons, currently our prison system is overwhelmingly a public prison system. At present, most prisoners (1,330,000) are housed in state prisons rather than federal ones, which house only 197,000 inmates.[43] But there is a mismatch in the way costs are calculated, since the counties sentence offenders to state prisons, but the states pay for the prisons, not the counties.[44] Thus, since they are not paying for the costs, the judges in the counties can readily sentence prisoners to harsher and longer sentences and the prosecutors can press for them, without factoring the cost of imprisonment into the punishment equation.

Efficiencies of long-term costs are also not taken into consideration in running the prisons, given that better treatment of prisoners could lead them to be more productive in prison work. Moreover, with better treatment, prisoners could have more opportunity to educate and improve themselves while in prison, resulting in reduced costs to them and their families if they can find more productive work when they get out. Such productive work would also result in reduced costs to taxpayers who would no longer have to pay to incarcerate them.

Regrettably, present prison conditions do not lend themselves to any such rosy scenario. Rather, nearly all our prisons emphasize the punishment of offenders and provide a very abusive and degrading environment, both in the way they are treated by corrections officer staff and by fellow

---

[43] Peter Wagner and Bernadette Rabuy, "Mass Incarceration: The Whole Pie 2017", Prison Policy Initiative, https://www.prisonpolicy.org/reports/pie2017.html
[44] Pfaff, *Locked In*, pp.142-143, 213

prisoners. Staff are often paid low salaries, experience bad encounters with inmates, and exhibit high turnover, 20-30% annually.[45] In turn, this high turnover contributes to the high cost of corrections, and a key factor of this high turnover is the oppressive prison environment that demoralizes the staff along with the prisoners. Short-term cost considerations trump possible long-term savings.

An example of how bad things can be is illustrated in the picture below. While individual cells are rarely as bad as this one, they can be.

Some prisons are also severely overcrowded and house prisoners together. Many in hot climates are not air conditioned.

---

[45] Jen Fifield, "Many States Face Dire Shortage of Prison Guards", Pew Charitable Trusts/Research & Analysis/Stateline, 3/1/2016.

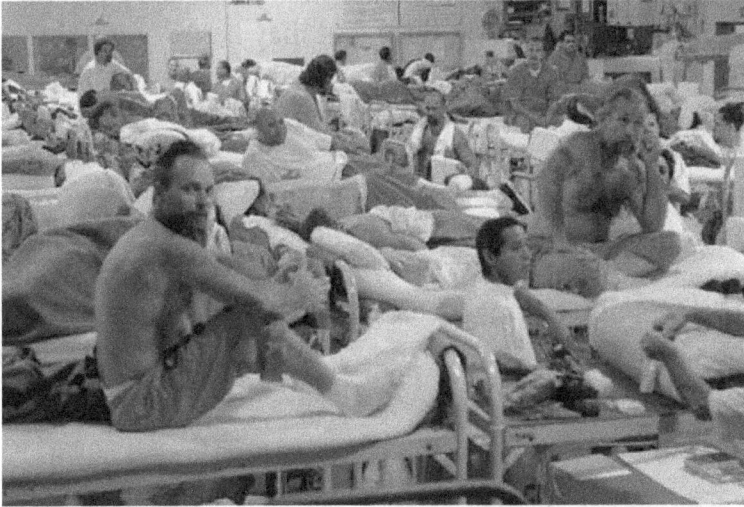

One harsh reality of prisons is that they contribute to racial conflict, not just between prisoners, but also with prison guards, the majority of whom are white due to the rural location of many prisons. Most of these guards know no blacks other than prisoners, which reinforces their feelings of superiority. In turn, their attitude probably contributes to the harsher disciplinary treatment black prisoners receive.

A second harsh reality is that prisons generate what prisoners consider a form of slave labor, where inmates work in "correctional industries" doing things like preparing license plates for wages that amount to an average of less than $3.50 a day, far below any minimum wage, and Alabama, Arkansas, Florida, Georgia and Texas don't pay inmates at all for regular prison jobs.[46] In California, female inmates fight fires for less than $2 an hour.[47]

---

[46] Wendy Sawyer, "How much do incarcerated people earn in each state?", Prison Policy Initiative Updates, 4/13/2017.
[47] James Lowe, "In the Line of Fire", *New York Times Magazine*, 9/3/2017

Such poor conditions may seem to reduce costs of imprisonment in the short term, but they have long term economic effects. While liberals might point to the harsh conditions being unjust or inhumane, there are strong economic considerations for improving conditions. Aside from the increased productivity of prisoners living under improved conditions and having more economic success when they get out, less racial friction and gang conflict is likely as conditions improve. So taking steps to improve the prison environment and the morale of prisoners can yield real economic benefits.

For now, though, prisons get away with these poor conditions because they enter into contracts to provide a certain number of units of a product for a very low price. They keep this price low by charging the inmates for their food and lodging and deducting this cost from the prisoner's already low cents per hour pay, leaving the prisoners with virtually nothing. Inmates go along with this mistreatment, because such "good behavior" may help shorten their sentences and provide them with training or a certain skill that might benefit them upon release.

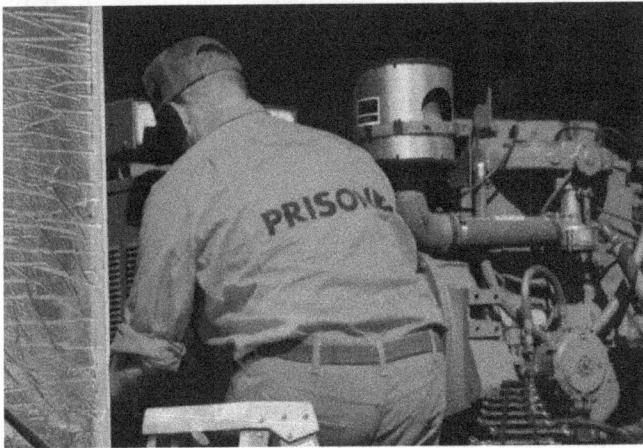

It is reasonable that a good proportion of the money the prisoners earn should be taken by the prison system for food and lodging. However, prisoners would be less resentful of the practice and better incentivized to work and rehabilitate themselves for eventual release, if they were allowed to keep more of their pay. This extra pay could then be kept in savings accounts that the prisoners can only access upon their release. The advantage of holding onto these funds is that they would make a significant difference in helping the prisoners successfully re-enter society.[48] Otherwise, if given the extra funds while in prison, the prisoners would be likely to spend it, leaving them with very limited funds upon their release -- a key factor in the return to crime of many

---

[48] However, the sum saved should be less than what an ex-con could save from working the same number of hours on a minimum wage job after being released. This is because the ex-con should always be incentivized to leave prison and work on the outside rather than succumbing to any temptation to remain in prison.

criminals. Currently, they simply don't have the funds, a job to go to, or family support to sustain them, so they return to what they have known in the past -- engaging in crime to make a living.

Solitary Confinement

Solitary confinement is another overused penalty in prison that adds unnecessary costs, too. Aside from the cost of keeping a prisoner in a solitary cell, there are extra costs in the loss of that person's prison labor and further costs from additional psychological support a prisoner long-held in solitary may need to readjust to being part of the general prison population. Here are the grim facts that support these observations.

Approximately 80,000 incarcerated individuals are held in solitary confinement, in individual cells by themselves 23 hours a day. They are allowed only one hour outside their cells for exercise and showers perhaps twice a week.[49]

Solitary confinement of this sort drives men mad. The absence of social interaction and any control over their own situations forces them inward. This is particularly difficult for men who are uncomfortable in their own skins, and it is an experience that many never recover from. Similar changes in behavior have been documented in monkeys kept for a time in solitary confinement.

Solitary confinement is utilized too frequently as an unnecessary and counterproductive form of punishment. It needs to be reserved as a last resort for inmates who are a serious risk to other inmates or prison staff. A Maine prison

---

[49] "Last Days of Solitary", *PBS, Frontline,* April 18, 2017

has managed to reduce its solitary confinement population by over 90% over a period of three years.[50]

Unfortunately, most individuals who work in the criminal justice system have little understanding of the ravages caused by solitary confinement, since they have not experienced this extreme isolation themselves. One official who did subject himself to this experience is former NYPD Commissioner Bernard Kerik, who subsequently recommended that others in the criminal justice system experience this. As he put it: "Every prosecutor, judge, correction officer and jail and prison official should have to spend 72 hours in the hole to see what it's like."[51]

Federal Prisons

One significant expense in the correction system involves a large number of prisoners convicted of drug offenses, especially in federal cases, where they wind up in federal prisons. While far fewer inmates are in federal prisons than in state prisons, a much greater percentage of them are there for drug crimes, as the following statistics show. Compared to the more than 1.3 million inmates housed in state prisons, less than 200,000 are housed in federal prisons, because they are sentenced there by a smaller number of federal courts for federal crimes. However, a much greater proportion of federal prison inmates are serving time for drug crimes than in state prisons, since a majority of them - 97,000 -- are serving time for drugs, while another 71,000 of them

---

[50] "Last Days of Solitary", *PBS, Frontline,* April 18, 2017
[51] Kerik, *From Jailer to Jailed,* p.60.

are there for public order crimes, like weapons and immigration.[52]

Unfortunately, the economic fallout from imprisonment is further compounded by housing young first time offenders with seasoned criminals in low security prisons. One result of this is that the old timers help to introduce the younger prisoners to the ways of prison life, so they are more likely to turn to crime rather than be productive when they are released -- an obvious drain on the financial system. This is a problem where Kerik has severely criticized the low security federal prisons for housing the first time and seasoned criminals together. It is, as he describes it, "a school for convicts."[53] It seems likely that this situation may occur in other prisons or jails, and should be further researched.

Private Prisons

In the short term, establishing private prisons has seemed like a good way to save money by reducing the costs of dealing with each prisoner. However, consequent reductions prisoner productivity, educational and job skill opportunities, employability when released lead to increased recidivism and more lawsuits. Thus, private prisons may actually result in higher long-term costs. The following discussion illustrates this dilemma of turning to private prisoners instead of trying to make the fixes needed in the public prisons and jails.

---

[52] Peter Wagner and Bernadette Rabuy, "Mass Incarceration: The Whole Pie 2017", Prison Policy Initiative, https://www.prisonpolicy.org/reports/pie2017.html
[53] Kerik, *From Jailer to Jailed*, pp. 258-9.

Private for-profit prisons have flourished in an environment where insufficient prison beds were available due to the high number of both state and federal prisoners. The overly long sentences for many crimes have contributed to the serious overcrowding problem in most prisons. At the same time, the budgets for prisons have gone down, resulting in a reduced level of care, as well as housing, at most prisons.

Given this dilemma of a higher prison population and less money and resources, the government found it easier to farm out the problem to the private sector without a huge rise in cost, since private contractors bid to build or staff prisons for less. Consequently, it appeared to be a seemingly easy, economical hand-off for the state and federal prison officials, although ultimately this short-term fix may have turned into a larger long-term economic cost. Presumably, this privatization approach meant that problems that arose in the prison – from routine operational difficulties to prison riots -- could be blamed on the private companies running the prisons. Yet, ultimately, in lawsuits, the state and federal employers have been sued for being responsible for the actions of the prison companies they hired, adding further to the long-term costs of incarceration.

The states have been responsible for the problems arising from hiring private contractors, since most private prisons are state prisons. Although California and Colorado are making moves to reduce their reliance on private prisons, most other states have not. Liberals and progressives are particularly perturbed by private prisons due to their concerns about mistreatment and prisoner abuse, though conservatives should be concerned, too, because of increased long-term costs.

A big problem is that for-profit private prisons are flawed by their business model. They can become more profitable if they provide the prisoners with less. In addition, their business model is based on a continuous desire to expand, but they can only do so if mass incarceration is increased, which is in the interests of private prison corporation shareholders but not in the interests of the country. In effect, liberals believe the private prison system poses the kind of concerns which President Eisenhower expressed in his warning about the dangers of an expanding military-industrial complex.[54]

Trump's election victory may represent a win for private prisons because of his "get tough on crime" approach.[55] Liberal fears about private prisons are overblown. That's because in spite of all the liberal rhetoric about them, only 8% of the prison population is housed in private prisons.

The Prison-Industrial Complex

Besides the long-term costs of incarceration in private prisons, there are other costs where the U.S. government, as well as prisoners and their families are being gouged. This is ultimately another increase in costs for the U.S. taxpayer and the economy. Let me explain.

While private prisons house relatively few prisoners, private companies own contracts for generating many prison products and for providing many prison services. Those companies are able to negotiate contracts with the prisons to provide items like license plates at very low cost because the

---

[54] Rebecca McCray, "Will States Follow Feds' Lead on Private Prisons?" *Takepart,* August 24, 2016;
http://www.takepart.com/article/2016/08/23/private-prisons-states
[55] Jeff Sommer, "Trump's win gives prison stocks a reprieve," *New York Times*, December 4, 2016.

prisoners are paid next to nothing at all. So prisoners are kept in a state of near slavery, making it more difficult for them to have the funds needed to support themselves after being released, so they are less able to become productive citizens and more likely to return to crime.

Additionally, private companies are allowed to charge outrageous rates for telephone calls between inmates and families and for all necessary personal hygiene and other items inmates must buy at the prison. The companies which provide food to prisons maximize their profits by providing the cheapest, and possibly least nutritious, food possible. The companies stocking commissaries and providing other services to prisoners likewise rake in the profits at inmates' and inmate families' expense. Many of these families have to rely on welfare support, so these outrageously high costs ultimately result in higher costs for taxpayers, too.

So why don't the state and federal government officials who negotiate these contracts seek a better deal? Why shouldn't they want to reduce costs, such as by bidding out prison food and other services to more companies? One good reason is that collusion between private companies and state legislatures runs deep,[56] and it does with corrupt prison officials, too.[57] What that means is that these politicians and prison officials can be getting kickbacks or other *quid per quo* exchanges to make it worthwhile for them to approve these excessively high priced contracts or look the other way.

---

[56] Daniel Wagner, "Profiting from Prisoners. Prison Bankers Cash in on Captive Customers. Inmates' Families Gouged by Fees", The Center for Public Integrity, 9/30/2014 & 11/11/2014;
https://www.publicintegrity.org/2014/09/30/15761/prison-bankers-cash-captive-customers
[57] FBI, "What We Investigate. Public Corruption",
https://www.fbi.gov/investigate/public-corruption

Prison Overcrowding and Riots

Prison overcrowding is another situation where there may seem to be lower costs, based on the notion of crowding more and more prisoners into the same physical space. After all, if you divide the same area by twice as many prisoners, that would seem to reduce the costs accordingly. But in fact, such overcrowding can contribute to increased costs, especially over the long-term, in numerous ways. Some of the fall-out might be increased medical costs due to serious illnesses, which are more likely to sweep through the prison population where overcrowding occurs. Other problems could be increases in physical confrontations between prisoners and each other and with guards, due to the stress of living in closer quarters. And the costs of mistreatment, prison riots, and lawsuits are an ever-present problem, too.

One example of such dangers that accompany overcrowding is a recent prison riot in Delaware that resulted in the death of a correctional officer. The prison was overcrowded, understaffed, and poorly run.[58]

An especially notorious example of the problems of overcrowding is the most tragic prison riot, which occurred at Attica in 1971, when about a thousand prisoners protesting prison conditions took hostages and rioted. After considerable negotiation, New York Governor Nelson Rockefeller called in the state police who stormed the prison. All told, 33 inmates and 10 correctional officers and civilian employees died.

The Attica riot ushered in an era of public fear and demand for more law and order, resulting in the building of

---

[58]Randall Chase, "Report on prison finds crowding, poor leadership. Delaware probing fatal riot", *Associated Press, Arkansas Democrat-Gazette*, 6/3/2017.

even more prisons to house the mushrooming number of convicts that resulted from nationwide crackdowns on crime, especially drugs.

Unfortunately, the popular TV series *Orange is the New Black* has sensationalized prison riots in its 2017 series, by making the prisoners seem more sympathetic and aligned against an unfair, repressive, and sometimes stupid and foolish prison administration. The program has been designed to appeal to a mostly liberal audience that typically takes the side of the convicts against the evil prison apparatus and staffing. What gets lost in these appeals is the value of correcting these ills for economic reasons and recognizing that some of the prisoners are there for a very good reason -- the serious crimes they committed and the need to protect the public from them committing such crimes in the future. However, the prisoners still need to be treated humanely and not subjected to overcrowding and abuse while in prison, for reasons previously discussed.

In any event, overcrowding is such a frequent complaint about prisons that it has been a major incentive for the call to build new prisons. Regrettably the other more cost-effective alternative has not gotten much consideration -- namely to reduce the number of unnecessary incarcerations so there is less overcrowding and therefore less need for expensive new prisons. Unfortunately, this call for building ever more prisons has the support of the prison industry and the politicians they help to reelect with their contributions, though as discussed, this option is bad for the taxpayers and the American economy as a whole.

Local Jails

Adding to the excessive costs is the high jail population, which includes many defendants who have not been convicted, but are simply waiting for their case to be adjudicated because they cannot afford bail. Here's a breakdown of the extent of the problem.

We have a staggering 11.6 million jail admissions each year![59] One reason this number is so high is that jail stays tend to be much shorter than prison stays, since the jail population consists of either defendants awaiting trial or convicts who are sentenced for up to one year for misdemeanor and felony verdicts. The jail population at any one moment in time is considerably lower than the prison population, but still significant.

Of the total admissions at any given time, local county jails house approximately 630,000 people, of which only 187,000 have been convicted. The remaining 443,000

---

[59] Peter K. Enns, *Incarceration Nation: How the United States Became the Most Punitive Democracy in the World*, Cambridge University Press, 2016, chapter 7.

arrestees[60] are held in these county jails for indeterminate times, because they fail to meet bail and because the justice system is so backed up that it takes weeks for a defendant to go to trial or even have his attorney work out and agree to a plea deal. This *in limbo* status unhinges many inmates who are awaiting a resolution for their case, particularly if they suffer from mental illness to begin with. As a consequence, the suicide rate of inmates is nearly five times that of the population at large, and is the leading cause of death among jail inmates.[61]

In turn, both mental illness and suicides generate additional costs to the prison system, from more medical expenses to the cost of investigations when there is a suicide, which in some cases turns out to be a homicide, resulting from a conflict between individuals or groups of inmates.

---

[60] Peter Wagner and Bernadette Rabuy, "Mass Incarceration: The Whole Pie 2017", Prison Policy Initiative,
https://www.prisonpolicy.org/reports/pie2017.html
[61] Prison Policy Initiative, 12/22/16.

Youth Detention

Approximately 34,000 inmates are detained in youth incarceration centers, the greatest proportion of which are for crimes against persons (13,600), followed by property crimes (8100), technical violations (6600), public order disturbances (3700) and drug crimes (1900). About 4500 youths are locked up in adult prisons or jails.[62]

---

[62] Peter Wagner and Bernadette Rabuy, "Mass Incarceration: The Whole Pie 2017", Prison Policy Initiative, https://www.prisonpolicy.org/reports/pie2017.html

The per person cost of juvenile detention is more than twice that of imprisoning adults, according to a study of mass incarceration by James Kilgore.[63]

---

[63] James Kilgore, *Understanding Mass Incarceration: A People's Guide to the Key Civil Rights Struggle of Our Time,* The New Press, 2015, p. 128.

Other Detentions

Still other costs in the criminal justice system are due to those detained by Immigration (41,000), or in territorial prisons (13,000), confined by civil commitment (6400), or jailed by the courts in Indian Country (2500) or by the military (1400).[64]

Immigration detention centers have mushroomed from just 18 centers with an average daily population of only 54 in 1981 to 204 centers with an average daily population of 32,095 in 2011.[65]

The Parole and Probation Systems

Many other countries don't have parole or probation systems. The difference between the U.S. and other countries is even more extreme than the differences in the charts on pages 15 and 16, if you add in those on parole and probation.[66]

---

[64] Peter Wagner and Bernadette Rabuy, "Mass Incarceration: The Whole Pie 2017", Prison Policy Initiative, https://www.prisonpolicy.org/reports/pie2017.html

[65] James Kilgore, *Understanding Mass Incarceration: A People's Guide to the Key Civil Rights Struggle of Our Time*, The New Press, 2015, p. 83.

[66] Data source: Department of Justice: http://www.ojp.doj.gov/bjs/correct.htm; International Centre for Prison Studies: http://www.kcl.ac.uk

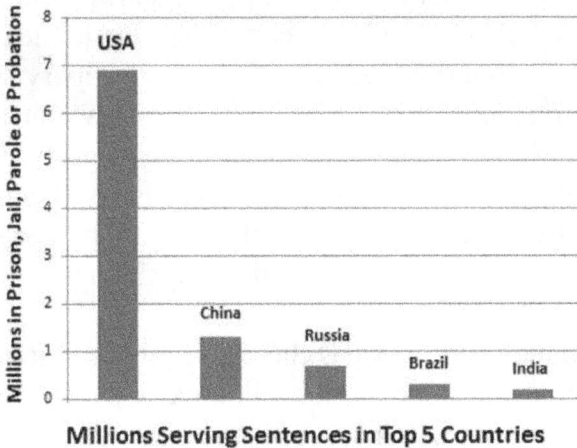

Millions Serving Sentences in Top 5 Countries

In fact, over half of those in correction in the world are serving sentences in the U.S. This horrific situation does have at least one very slim silver lining for an offender and another for taxpayers. For offenders, it is better to be on parole or probation, since these offer more freedom than being confined in a prison or jail cell. For taxpayers, the cost of supervision on parole or probation is considerably less than the cost of prison or jail. However, despite these savings, we skimp too much on parole and probation supervision. As a result, the parole and probation systems are both understaffed.

Because both the parole and probation systems are understaffed, the caseloads for both parole and probation officers are well above those that are recommended.[67,68,69]

---

[67] It is very difficult to get national statistics regarding caseloads and turnover, so I have had to resort to using results from individual states.

[68] Cathy Frye, "Parole officers feeling the heat. Heavy caseloads ramp up stress; job turnover high", *Northwest Arkansas Democrat-Gazette*, 8/25/13.

[69] "Probation and Parole: A Primer for Law Enforcement Officers", Bureau of Justice Assistance, U.S. Department of Justice, 2009.

This understaffing has several important detrimental economic as well as social consequences. First, understaffing means that felons are not adequately enough supervised to prevent them from committing new crimes -- which can be very costly. Second, understaffing results in caseworker stress and burnout, which adds costs because of the need to train new caseworkers because of the very high rates of turnover, 20-30% nationally,[70] and nearly 50% here in the Little Rock area.[71]

Such high turnover has the consequence that new caseworkers, usually inexperienced, have to supervise the parolees. For parolees, this is a clear disadvantage, because the continuity of their supervision is disrupted, with negative results. Frequently, they have to start over from scratch with their new parole officer, which can be very destabilizing for their reintegration back into the community. As a result, they may be more likely to reconnect with their old buddies with criminal records and return to crime.

One way to help convicts returning to the community readjust and avoid returning to crime is greater cooperation between parole and probation officers and the local police. For example, the parole or probation officer can make unannounced visits, as in Boston. Then, should the parole or probation officer notice anything suspicious, he or she can alert the local police or take other proactive action to help the ex-convict avoid engaging in criminal activity. However,

---

[70]Len Sipes, Kirsten Lewis and Adam Matz, "Stress and Turnover in Parole and Probation-APPA"; http://media.csosa.gov/podcast/audio/2014/03/stress-turnover-parole-and-probation-appa

[71] Cathy Frye, "Parole officers feeling the heat. Heavy caseloads ramp up stress; job turnover high", *Northwest Arkansas Democrat-Gazette*, 8/25/13.

though parole and probation supervision would represent a cost-effective way to better monitor ex-convicts and steer them away from criminal activity,[72] not many communities use that approach.

Parole

The parole system is designed to take effect after time in prison, and it currently keeps 840,000 felons[73] under the supervision of 11,000 parole officers[74] attached to courts around the U.S.

Parole officers have to assess the living environment of parolees and often do so in unannounced visits. In many cases, the parole system is able to provide a degree of re-entry training and advice to try to keep the ex-con from committing more crime. As such, it is a mix of rehabilitation coupled with lesser punishment than prison.

The parole system is a victim of excessive budgetary restrictions and mismanagement. Done well, parole can reduce recidivism. However, when the system is overloaded because it doesn't have enough caseworkers, it will save a state some money, compared to sending a convict to prison, but it won't reduce recidivism (repeat offenses by ex-cons). An overloaded parole system fails to reduce recidivism because a caseworker with too many cases to handle is unable

---

[72] "Probation and Parole: A Primer for Law Enforcement Officers," Bureau of Justice Assistance, U.S. Department of Justice, 2009.
[73] Peter Wagner and Bernadette Rabuy, "Mass Incarceration: The Whole Pie 2017", Prison Policy Initiative, https://www.prisonpolicy.org/reports/pie2017.html
[74] Len Sipes, Kirsten Lewis and Adam Matz, "Stress and Turnover in Parole and Probation-APPA"; http://media.csosa.gov/podcast/audio/2014/03/stress-turnover-parole-and-probation-appa

to provide the necessary supervision to help an ex-con avoid turning back to crime. Thus inadequate supervision eventually leads back to prison for many ex-cons.

Statistics clearly show how much caseworkers are overwhelmed with too many cases, many of them high risk, with a need for even closer supervision. The recommended guidelines are 20 high-risk cases per parole officer or 40 cases which are considered low or medium risk. In California, 63% of parole agents had caseloads above those levels.[75] By these standards, the 11,000 parole officers nationally would at most be able to handle 440,000 of the 840,000 felons.

In some states there are even policies that turn parole officers into financial collection agents. This compromises their ability to effectively supervise parolees. For example, in Arkansas, parole officers are also required to collect 80% of

---

[75] Adolfo Flores, "More than 60% of state parole agents' caseloads exceed policy limits", *Los Angeles Times*, 12/5/2014.

supervision fees from parolees.[76] This puts great pressure on both parolees, who may be penniless, and parole officers. These charges could actually lead parolees to commit crimes to get the funds to pay for their supervision -- an example of the system undermining its own purpose.

Unlike prisons, jails and probation, the numbers of parolees has not declined in recent years.[77]

Probation

The probation department similarly suffers from too many cases per officer and mismanagement. The probation system exists in parallel with the prison system and it is designed for individuals who are convicted of less serious offenses. Instead of going to prison or jail, convicts are sentenced to serve their time outside of prison or jail but under probation. Besides providing less severe punishment for lesser crimes, the system was designed to relieve pressure on the overcrowded prison and jail systems.

There are far more people on probation (3,700,000)[78] than on parole, in prison or in jail, and they are supervised by only 60,000 probation officers.[79] Unfortunately, the caseload for probation officers may also be too high to keep recidivism

---

[76] Cathy Frye, "Parole officers feeling the heat. Heavy caseloads ramp up stress; job turnover high", *Northwest Arkansas Democrat-Gazette,* 8/25/13.

[77] Wendy Sawyer, "Probation population declines: Good but not good enough", Prison Policy Initiative Updates, 12/22/2016.

[78] Peter Wagner and Bernadette Rabuy, "Mass Incarceration: The Whole Pie 2017", Prison Policy Initiative, https://www.prisonpolicy.org/reports/pie2017.html

[79] "Probation and Parole: A Primer for Law Enforcement Officers", Bureau of Justice Assistance, U.S. Department of Justice, 2009.

down: a study in Iowa found a 47% decrease in recidivism for property or violent crime when probation officer caseload was reduced 40%.[80] However, these caseloads have not been reduced more generally.

Community supervision of those on probation primarily has decreased from 2215 supervised per 100,000 U.S. adults in 2005 to 1868 supervised in 2015.[81] Although the numbers of those on probation have begun to decline since 2007,[82] almost twice as many people are on probation as are in prison or jail. Sentencing an individual to serve time on probation rather than going to prison is far less expensive to taxpayers and much better than prison for offenders. Even so, their lives are severely restricted by having to report regularly – usually once a week – to their probation officer. They are also subject to checks of their home and car at will, should their probation officer suspect they might be involved in some nefarious criminal activity. Another risk they face, should they violate probation, is the possibility that a judge will send them to prison to serve out the rest of their sentence, or give them a longer sentence, which can be served in prison, on probation, or both. Yet, on balance, putting convicts on probation rather than sending them to jail is more cost-effective, and any programs to reduce the caseload of probation officers would contribute significantly to reducing recidivism and therefore the costs of crime.

---

[80] "Program Profile: Reduced Probation Caseload in Evidence-Based Setting (Iowa)", National Institute of Justice, July 17, 2012, https://www.crimesolutions.gov/ProgramDetails.aspx?ID=259
[81] Danielle Kaeble and Thomas P. Bonczar, "Probation and Parole in the United States, 2015 ", U.S. Department of Justice, Office of Justice Programs, 12/2016, revised 2/2/2017.
[82] Wendy Sawyer, "Probation population declines: Good but not good enough", Prison Policy Initiative Updates, 12/22/2016.

Different Types of Prisoners

It is also important to consider the different types of prisoners in deciding what to do to fix our prisons.

Prisoners over 50 substantially drive up healthcare costs to prisons, and they are far less likely to commit crimes. It would be well worthwhile to consider early parole for older prisoners, particularly if they have a family or other support structure available to them on the outside. They are far less likely to commit crimes than younger offenders. The age of maximum criminal activity is 18-20, and criminal activity declines precipitously and continuously with increasing age. However, there is a significant cohort of older people committing crimes.[83]

The mentally ill and addicted represent another category of prisoners which abound in prisons. As a result of new policies enacted in the 1960s by John F. Kennedy[84] to send patients to their communities where trained professionals would take better care of them, the population of the mentally ill in state mental institutions plummeted from 560,000 in 1955 to 160,000 in 1976.[85] However, the local communities were ill-equipped to handle them, and prisons have become the repositories for the mentally ill. Moreover, the prisons are ill-equipped to deal with them. Ten times as many mentally ill are incarcerated in prison as in state

---

[83] Pfaff, *Locked In*, 2017, p. 75.

[84] on account of what had happened due to a lobotomy of his sister Rosemary

[85] "A History of Mental Institutions in the United States", *TikiToki*; http://www.tiki-toki.com/timeline/entry/37146/A-History-of-Mental-Institutions-in-the-United-States/#vars!date=1874-02-17_16:12:32!

hospitals.[86] There are only one-tenth the number of psychiatric hospital beds as there used to be in 1955.[87] The closing of abhorrent mental institutions was originally viewed as an advance, but putting the mentally ill who pled guilty to crimes in prison was not a suitable substitute. Also, releasing a huge number of mentally ill from prison put many of them on the street, since they were unable to hold jobs and had unstable family environments. On the street they became part of a low-income and often homeless group, sometimes resorting to criminal activity.

This problem of the mentally ill in prison is huge. Nationwide, 15% of male inmates and over 30% of female inmates have serious mental illness.[88] Research studies have shown that about 15% of inmates have less severe mental health issues, 25% have substance abuse issues, and 40% have both.[89] Representative Tim Murphy (R-Pa) claims that the majority of those in state and local jails have a mental disorder.[90] The percentage of male and female inmates with at least one mental health problem in different kinds of institutions is shown in the table below.[91]

---

[86] "Sweden Has Done for Its Prisoners What the U.S. Won't," https://mic.com/articles/109138/sweden-has-done-for-its-prisoners-what-the-u-s-won-t#.rKzDsN58s

[87] E. Fuller Torrey, Aaron D. Kennard, Don Eslinger, Richard Lamb and James Pavle, "More Mentally Ill Persons Are in Jail and Prisons Than Hospitals: A Survey of the States", Treatment Advocacy Center, May, 2010.

[88] "Unnecessarily Incarcerated," Brennan Center, https://www.brennancenter.org/sites/default/files/publications/Unnecessarily_Incarcerated.pdf

[89] Ibid., Fig. 6.

[90] PBS News Hour, 12/13/2016.

[91] Sarah Varney, "By the numbers: Mental illness behind bars", *PBS News Hour* 5/15/2014.

	Male inmates with at least one mental health problem	Female inmates with at least one mental health problem
State prisons	55%	73%
Federal prisons	44%	61%
Local jails	63%	75%

About one-third of the homeless have serious mental illness,[92] putting them at great risk of recidivism.

While solitary confinement is used for the most dangerous prisoners or as a disciplinary tool by the guards to gain prisoner acquiescence to prison rules, it costs a lot more than regular incarceration and can be enough to drive men insane, particularly the mentally ill. As mentioned earlier, solitary confinement should be used as a last resort, not as a means of punishment for misbehavior.

The Los Angeles County jail system, which has the largest jail system in the U.S., houses the largest population of mentally ill in the country. It has 4500 mentally ill out of a total inmate population of 18,000 – 25% of the total population. Imprisoning mentally ill inmates tends to have a high cost because of their special needs. For one thing, they need to be checked on every 15 minutes for risk of suicide. They also need to be treated for their mental illness. Since over 30% of use of force cases in jails in L.A. involve inmates with mental illness, a new staff training program emphasizes using communication rather than force to de-escalate situations.[93]

---

[92] Treatment Advocacy Center, "Eliminating Barriers to the Treatment of Mental Illness", 7/25/2014.
[93] "This is Life with Lisa Ling", 12/23/2016

Similar problems exist nationally. As reported in a national survey, 75% of inmates were involved with drug or alcohol problems at time of their arrest, and the percentage may even be higher with female inmates.[94]

Thus, the mentally ill might be better served in professionally staffed treatment facilities outside of prison or jail. Former NYPD Commissioner under Rudy Giuliani, Bernard Kerik agrees with this reassignment. As he flatly states: "People who need treatment for drug or mental health problems do not belong in prison. They belong in treatment centers."[95]

Prisoners with learning or cognitive disabilities also fill up the prisons because they lack the skills needed to get a job. Because of these disabilities, many prisoners had to repeat grades and become high school dropouts at higher risk for incarceration. Learning disabilities include dyslexia[96] (the most prevalent, making reading extremely difficult) and attention deficit hyperactivity disorder (ADHD).[97]

According to recent research, approximately 5-17% of the population have dyslexia, which can be treated, but few individuals get treated for it. For example, in Arkansas, only about 10% of those with the problem receive treatment, and most students in poorer school districts do not. This condition, if untreated, can, in turn, lead to crime and is common in prison and jail inmates. About 2 in 10 prisoners have a cognitive disability (four times that of the general

[94] K.L. Cropsey et al. "Specialized Prisons and Services: Results from a National Survey," *Prison Journal*, 87, 58-85, 2007
[95] Bernard B. Kerik, *From Jailer to Jailed*, p. 280.
[96] Benjamin Hardy, "Dyslexia dysfunction", *Arkansas Times*, 6/9/2016.
[97] National Center for Learning Disabilities, "The State of Learning Disabilities", 2014.

population), as do 3 in 10 jail inmates (six times that of the general population).[98]

The percentage of Americans with learning disabilities is higher in males (2%) and higher still among those living in poverty. But getting treatment and special education can help to give poor learners the ability to get an education and a job, leading to more productive citizens and reduced crime. For example, participating in treatment and special education programs has contributed to 68% of those with learning disabilities finishing high school in 2011. In this regard, it is well known that high school graduates are less prone to crime than high school dropouts.

Such programs can have a major positive impact, since there are 2.4 million public school students with learning disabilities (about 5% of total enrollment or 41% of special education enrollment), and two-thirds of them are male, with blacks and Hispanics overrepresented. Only 52% of black and 55% of Hispanic students with disabilities completed high school with a regular degree in 2011. In addition, less than half of working age adults with learning disabilities are employed. Another shocking statistic is that 55% of people with learning disabilities encountered the criminal justice system within eight years of leaving high school (stopped by police, arrested, jailed, on parole or on probation).

Intervention to help individuals with cognitive disabilities can have a major deterrent effect on crime. For instance, youths who had jobs or attended high school within six months of release from a correctional facility were 3.2

---

[98] Jennifer Bronson, Laura M. Maruschak and Marcus Berzofsky, "Disabilities Among Prison and Jail Inmates," U.S. Department of Justice, Special Report, December 2015.

times less likely to become recidivists.[99] Thus, there is a clear economic benefit from providing this treatment and special education.

Since dyslexia can be treated, it is imperative that dyslexics, especially young blacks who are more prone to the condition than other racial groups, be identified at an early age. Then, they can be given treatment before they fall so far behind their classmates that they drop out of school in disgust or despair and become more prone to criminal activities. Fortunately, the percent of those with learning disabilities who dropped out of school dropped from 35% in 2002 to 19% in 2011.[100]

Since treatment is possible and over half of those with learning disabilities encountered the criminal justice system within 8 years of leaving high school,[101] it would certainly represent a plus for conservatives if Education Secretary Betsy DeVos and Attorney General Jeff Sessions collaborated on programs to reduce the influence of dyslexia on juvenile crime.

Gang members represent another category of prisoners. More gangs operate in Los Angeles than anywhere else. Half of all state prison inmates in L.A. are gang members, and a quarter of all inmates are targets of the members of other gangs, so those groups need to be segregated from each other.[102]

---

[99] National Center for Learning Disabilities, "The State of Learning Disabilities", 2014; https://www.understood.org/~/media/e7fe0b6d28154101b2f55c89bf90b4ab.pdf

[100] Ibid.

[101] Ibid.

[102] "This is Life with Lisa Ling", 12/23/2016.

While counseling sessions are available to reduce recidivism, the gangs prevent their male members from participating in these programs because members of different gangs are mixed together for such sessions. Evidently, the prisons have no facilities to permit further segregation during group support sessions or they aren't willing to provide separate counseling sessions for members of individual gangs. As a result, male inmates who are most likely to be in gangs tend to avoid these programs, while female inmates, less likely to be in gangs, more often participate in counseling sessions.[103]

Gang violence occurs in the prisons, and gang leaders in prison direct those outside to engage in gang violence against opposing gang members as well as participate in organized criminal activity. In effect, criminal activity increased by incarceration has become an alternate form of business enterprise in lieu of other meaningful opportunities for financial success. Thus, a key remedy for the criminal

[103] Ibid.

justice system involves making some fixes in the prisons to undercut these roots of expanded criminal activity.

   Women in prison (8%) are far outnumbered by men (92%) in prison,[104] but they cost more to house and they cost society much more, because 60% of the women in state prisons are mothers of children under 18.[105] The societal costs are staggering, since the loss of a mom can hardly be replaced. Fractured families are the result of a mom in prison, with children suffering the most, often being raised by grandparents or other relatives, for whom the kids are an unanticipated burden. Others face difficult adjustments in foster homes.[106]

   However, children suffer when any parent is in prison, which tears at the very fabric of society. For once, Obama

[104] Rutgers University Camden, "Children and Families of the Incarcerated Fact Sheet," 2014; https://nrccfi.camden.rutgers.edu/files/nrccfi-fact-sheet-2014.pdf
[105] Nicholas Kristof, "Mothers in Prison," *New York Times*, 11/27/2016.
[106] Kathryn Joyce, "Mother and Child Disunion," *Arkansas Times*, 6/9/2016.

said it well in 2015 when he stated: "Mass incarceration rips apart families. It hollows out neighborhoods. It perpetuates poverty." This problem of parents in prison is especially great for blacks, since 11% of black children have a parent in prison. Though he is no fan of Obama's on other issues, Kerik agrees that we have not focused enough attention on the collateral damage done to offenders (never being able to cast off their ex-felon status).[107] In fact, this collateral damage extends to their families, and even society (the decline of urban black communities) and country (over-incarceration of individuals who could instead become productive citizens if given the skills and a job opportunity).

Further contributing to this breakup of families is the fact that over 60% of parents are held in prison over 100 miles away from their residence, which makes visiting difficult. As a result, more than 58% of prisoners receive

---

[107] Kerik, *From Jailer to Jailed,* p. 264.

no personal visits from their children.[108] Those that do receive visits are often ashamed to face their children or relatives.

The economic costs due to the over incarceration of blacks is especially great. Per capita, blacks are far more likely to be imprisoned than whites due to committing more crime and experiencing higher arrest and conviction rates, accompanied by sentencing to longer prison terms for equivalent offenses. Nearly one million of our 2.3 million incarcerated prisoners in the U.S. are black.[109] In fact, our prisons hold a much higher percent of our black population than blacks experienced in apartheid South Africa.[110] More blacks are under criminal supervision today than were enslaved before the Civil War.[111] The incarceration rate for blacks is more than 5 times higher than for whites nationwide, and in a few northern states, (Connecticut, Illinois, Iowa, Minnesota, New Jersey, Pennsylvania, and Wisconsin) the black incarceration rate is more than 10 times that of whites.[112,113] According to the 50 state average, 1.5% of all

---

[108] "Children and Families of the Incarcerated Fact Sheet," Rutgers University Camden, 2014; https://nrccfi.camden.rutgers.edu/files/nrccfi-fact-sheet-2014.pdf
https://www.hrw.org/reports/2000/usa/Rcedrg00-01.htm
[109] "NAACP Criminal Justice Fact Sheet,"
http://www.naacp.org/criminal-justice-fact-sheet/
[110] "Sweden Has Done for Its Prisoners What the U.S. Won't," https://mic.com/articles/109138/sweden-has-done-for-its-prisoners-what-the-u-s-won-t#.rKzDsN58s
[111]Baz Dreisinger, *Incarceration Nations*, Other Press, 2016, p.8.
[112]"Sentencing Project," http://www.sentencingproject.org/the-facts/#rankings?dataset-option=BWR
[113] "United States, Punishment and Prejudice: Racial Disparities in the War on Drugs. III. Incarceration and Race", Human Rights Watch, 2000; https://www.hrw.org/reports/2000/usa/Rcedrg00-01.htm

blacks are incarcerated at any given time, compared to less than 0.2% of whites.[114] Blacks make up 13% of the general population but over 37% of the prison population.[115] And 11% of 20-34 year old blacks are now in prison.[116] In 1995, one third of all black men aged 20-29 were in prison, jail or on probation or parole.[117]

Blacks are more likely to be in prison than other groups for a number of reasons. They are sent to prison for drug offenses at ten times the rate of whites, for which they serve nearly as long a term in prison as whites do for violent offenses.[118] Black males under 35 without a high school degree are more likely to be behind bars than to have a job.[119]

In fact, the rate of incarceration for blacks is so high that over their lifetime, one-third of black males will experience prison. And once in prison, even in a blue state like New York, they experience strong racial bias with excessive use of force by corrections officers.[120] Attica's

---

[114] Ibid.

[115] E. A. Carson, "Prisoners in 2013." Washington, DC: Department of Justice, Bureau of Justice Statistics; 2014

[116] Marc Lamont Hill, *Nobody: Casualties of America's War on the Vulnerable, from Ferguson to Flint and Beyond*, Atria Books, 2017, p. 123.

[117] "United States, Punishment and Prejudice: Racial Disparities in the War on Drugs. III. Incarceration and Race", Human Rights Watch, 2000; https://www.hrw.org/reports/2000/usa/Rcedrg00-01.htm

[118] "Criminal Justice Fact Sheet", NAACP; https://www.naacp.org/pages/criminal-justice-fact-sheet

[119] *The Growth of Incarceration in the United States: Exploring Causes and Consequences*, Chapter 1.

[120] "The Scourge of Racial Bias in New York State's Prisons," *New York Times*, December 4, 2016.

2240 inmates are mostly black and Hispanic, but they are overseen by 600 guards, nearly all of whom are white.[121]

Hispanics represent another significant prison population, one that is incarcerated in prisons or jails at a somewhat greater rate (22%) than their presence in the U.S. population as a whole (15.5%).[122] They also contribute significantly to the problem of gangs, both in and out of prisons, particularly in Los Angeles, and much of the same issues raised about the cost of African American criminal activity can apply to them.

A particular concern is the growing number of Hispanic convicts in the prisons, since the total number of Hispanic prisoners increased by nearly 125,000 between 2000

---

[121] Marc Lamont Hill, *Nobody: Casualties of America's War on the Vulnerable, from Ferguson to Flint and Beyond,* Atria Books, *2017, p. 148.*

[122] E. Ann Carson, "Prisoners in 2013," US Department of Justice Bulletin, 9/30/14, NCJ 247282, Table 7, https://bjs.gov/content/pub/pdf/p13.pdf

and 2011. By contrast, the number of white prisoners increased less than 30,000, and black prisoners actually decreased over 17,000 over that same period.[123]

Similar observations led the authors of *The Growth of Incarceration in the United States: Exploring Causes and Consequences* to conclude that minorities were much more likely to be incarcerated. As they stated in their conclusion:

> "People who live in poor and minority communities have always had substantially higher rates of incarceration than other groups. As a consequence, the effects of harsh penal policies in the past 40 years have fallen most heavily on blacks and Hispanics, especially the poorest."[124]

Summing Up

❖ **observations**

➢ **recommendations**

<u>Reduce the Prison Population Through Probation and Parole</u>

❖ We incarcerate too many of our citizens.

❖ This high rate of incarceration costs far too much financially and in terms of our international image.

---

[123] James Kilgore, *Understanding Mass Incarceration: A People's Guide to the Key Civil Rights Struggle of Our Time*, The New Press, 2015, p. 83.
[124] Jeremy Travis, Bruce Western and Steve Redburn, Editors, *The Growth of Incarceration in the United States: Exploring Causes and Consequences*, National Academies Press, 2014, p. 340.

❖ Too many of those in jails have not been convicted.

➢ Probation and parole are ways to reduce the prison population for those who have committed less serious crimes, and costs are much less than for imprisonment.

➢ Since caseworkers are overwhelmed with too many cases to supervise them adequately, reduce caseworker caseloads by reducing sentences and by hiring more caseworkers.

Move the Mentally Ill to Other Facilities

❖ Too many of those incarcerated are elderly with costly health problems.

❖ Too many of those incarcerated are mentally ill.

➢ The mentally ill could be better served in other facilities that could provide them with better treatment at a lower cost.

Reduce the Number of Prisoners with Problems of Substance Abuse or Learning Disabilities

❖ Too many of those incarcerated have substance abuse problems requiring treatment, but they generally don't receive it. They emerge from prison with substance abuse problems that increase their chances of being arrested and winding up back in prison.

❖ Many of the incarcerated have learning disabilities that may have contributed to school drop-out and lack of a job, which put them at increased risk for incarceration.

  ➢ Greater access to special education should be provided for those with limited means, particularly from minority communities that are disproportionately represented in prison. Those with learning disabilities in prison should be provided education in remedial reading and writing skills and encouraged to work toward a GED.

❖ Too many of those incarcerated are blacks or Hispanics, who are disproportionately more likely to be arrested, convicted and receive longer sentences.

  ➢ Recommendations that will address our overcrowded prisons will be found in the Chapters to follow.

❖ Families of those incarcerated are seriously adversely affected, with the greatest effects on black society.

  ➢ Efforts are needed to encourage continued contact of prisoners with their families and to help them gain skills while in prison and find productive work after getting out. These actions will contribute to family stability and reintegrating from prison into society upon release.

CHAPTER 3 – HOW OTHER COUNTRIES DEAL WITH PRISONS AND RECIDIVISM

One of the most shameful aspects of prisons in the U.S. is that we incarcerate a far higher proportion of our population than *any* other country, six times more than the average in Europe. As Obama and African-American and liberal researchers are fond of pointing out, we have 5% of the world's population but 25% of its prisoners, with 2.2 million in prison or jail in the U.S. alone. [125,126]

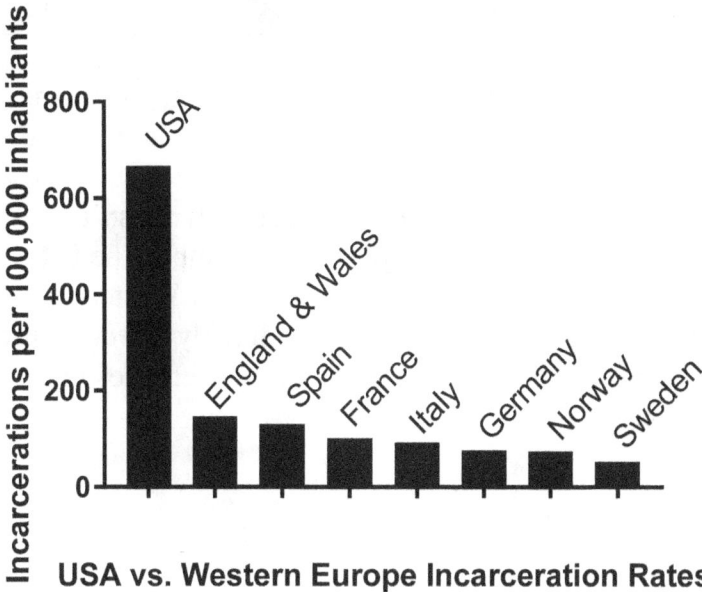

USA vs. Western Europe Incarceration Rates

[125] Barack Obama, "America is home to 5% of the world's population, but 25% of the world's prisoners," *Twitter*, 7/14/2015.
https://twitter.com/potus44/status/621081946236563456?lang=en
[126] "NAACP, Criminal Justice Fact Sheet," 2009,
http://www.naacp.org/criminal-justice-fact-sheet

Although we pay more per U.S. citizen (*per capita*) for prisons than European countries like Switzerland and Sweden, curiously, our total costs *per capita* are not double that of Sweden and are even lower than those of Switzerland:[127]

	U.S.	Switzerland	Sweden
police	215	280	165
prosecutors	12	17	10
court	80	87	11
prison	91	71	51
TOTAL	398	455	237

Considering the number of our prisoners, we manage to keep them incarcerated quite efficiently from a financial perspective.

Unfortunately, our higher incarceration doesn't translate into lower crime statistics. For example, the U.S. murder rate is significantly higher than that of Western European countries, which have a considerably lower murder rate than that of the U.S.,[128] similar to the differences in incarceration rates.

---

[127] Graham Farrell and Ken Clark, "What Does the World Spend on Criminal Justice?", The European Institute for Crime Prevention and Control, HEUNI paper No. 20, 2004 http://www.heuni.fi/material/attachments/heuni/papers/6KtlkZMtL/HEUNI_papers_20.pdf

[128] NationMaster "Crime > Violent crime > Murder rate per million people: Countries Compared" http://www.nationmaster.com/country-info/stats/Crime/Violent-crime/Murder-rate-per-million-people

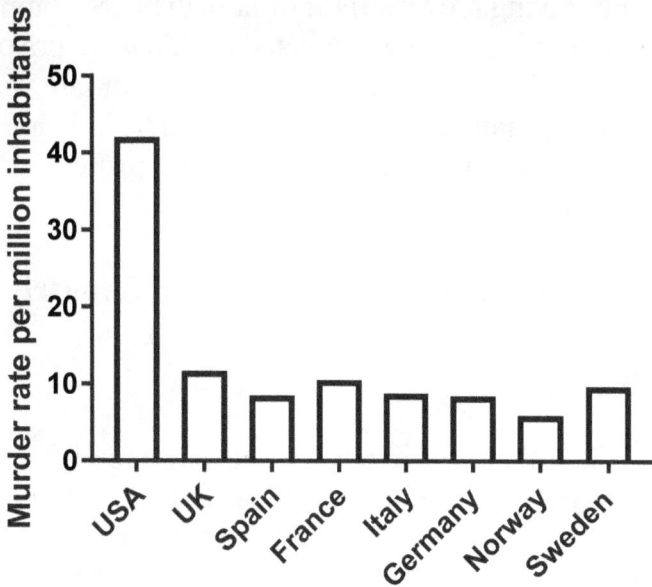

However, as later comparisons with other countries will show, murder rates do not justify the high rates of incarceration in the U.S.

Our prisons may be of higher quality than those in many Third World countries, but they do not compare well with those in many European countries. And we imprison far more people per capita than Russia or China, countries we consider to have terrible human rights records. What does that say about us? In *American Justice?,* I characterized the U.S. prison system as a national shame. In addition, our incarceration rates have high economic costs that are much higher than they need to be to keep us safe. Instead, the money wasted on prisons could go to a much more worthy approach, such as making the much needed improvements of our infrastructure, improving our schools, lowering our national debt, or improving other aspects of our broken criminal justice system.

Following are examples of how the U.S. compares to other countries in putting convicted criminals in prison, and as case after case illustrates, the U.S. does not fare well. These other countries might serve as models in helping us bring much needed reform to our criminal justice system.

Examples of Prisons in Other Countries

Europe

While the U.S. represents one extreme of incarceration, **Norway** represents the opposite extreme. Guards there carry no weapons, prisoners wear no uniforms, and the courts are less punitive. The longest prison sentence, even for mass murderer Anders Breivik, is only 21 years, although it could be lengthened by increments later.[129] Most Norwegian prisons are "open" and seem like country clubs to us.[130]

---

[129]"Why Norway's Prison System Is So Successful," *Business Insider*, December 12, 2016.http://www.businessinsider.com/why-norways-prison-system-is-so-successful-2014-12
[130] Photo courtesy Alex Masi.

They permit their inmates considerable freedom within the confines of the prison perimeter, allow them to cook their own meals, and provide them with considerable work training to prepare them for release. They even allow them to leave prison for work.

The prisons in Norway are small and located all around the country, and they allow prisoners to visit their families.[131]

Their prison cells look like dorm cells at a college. In some instances, they even have private bathrooms.

---

[131] Charles R. Larson,"Prisoner rehabilitation around the World", *Counterpunch*; http://www.counterepunch.org/2016/02/26/prisoner-rehabilitation-around-the-world

Norwegian prisons have these characteristics because the criminal justice system there emphasizes rehabilitation over punishment. One Republican congressman from Idaho noted the value of this approach when he asked, "What kind of person do we want leaving our prisons?" after he visited a Norwegian prison. Other officials from Idaho, North Dakota and Pennsylvania became convinced that our prisons can be made more humane,[132,133] leading to better consequences upon prisoner release, since the recidivism rate in Norway and the rest of Scandinavia is far lower than ours. In response, these states have each been adopting some Norwegian prison principles.

Even Scandinavian high security prisons are less punitive than ours. As a result, it is easier for Scandinavian prisoners to take responsibility and blame themselves for their plight, rather than blaming other individuals, their disadvantages growing up, the prison environment, or society in general, as U.S. prisoners often do. Thus, Scandinavian prisoners are better able to express remorse and seek to change themselves to improve their lives upon release.[134]

Still, not all Scandinavian prisons meet these high standards, so some prisons are showcased to visitors from other countries and others are not. Furthermore, as effective as the prison system in Norway may seem, it would not work

---

[132] "Idaho Prison Chief Takes Lesson from Abroad," *Arkansas Democrat-Gazette*, November 26, 2016.
[133] Tu-Uyen Tran, "Here's what Norway can Teach North Dakota About Prisons", *West Fargo Pioneer*, 2/8/2017; http://www.westfargopioneer.com/news/4214657-heres-what-norway-can-teach-north-dakota-about-prisons
[134] Doran Larson, "Why Scandinavian Prisons are Superior", *The Atlantic*, 9/24/2013; http://www.theatlantic.com/international/archive/2013/09/why-scandinavian-prisons-are-superior/279949

in the U.S., at least not on a mass scale, for two major reasons. One key reason is that Norwegian prisons don't have to deal with gang problems so prevalent in the U.S. This suggests that we should consider segregating gang members in different prisons. A second and even greater reason is that Norway spends three times more money per prisoner than we do,[135] and conservative Americans are not amenable to such treatment of prisoners at taxpayer expense, particularly to those of a different race or ethnicity who might be dangerous or undeserving. Yet one lesson that might be learned from Norwegian and other similar Scandinavian prisons is that prisoners given sufficient positive reinforcement and skills have a much greater chance of succeeding upon release.

Prisons in **Germany** are more similar to the Scandinavian model than to ours. Fewer of those convicted are sent to prison. Only about 5% wind up in prison, according to a report from a delegation that included conservatives from the Charles Koch Institute and the evangelical Prison Fellowship.[136] Many more prisoners receive sentences in the form of fines, which are assigned based in part on the offender's ability to pay. These fines keep them working. Up to one-third of the prisoners pay a

---

[135] Rakesh Sharma, "3 Reasons This 'Perfect' Prison System Will Not Work in America", *The CheatSheet*, 5/22/2015; http://www.cheatsheet.com/business/3-reasons-why-norways-prison-system-should-not-be-replicated-in-america.html/?a=viewall
[136] Nicholas Turner and Jeremy Travis, "What We Learned from German Prisons", *New York Times*, 8/6/2015.

"transaction" fee to avoid criminal prosecution, which has the same effect.[137]

Another big perk of the German prison system is that many of the prisoners are allowed out to work in the daytime and to visit friends and families several times a year.[138] Prison sentences are frequently suspended into a form of probation, and tasks are assigned similar to U.S. requirements for community service.[139] Of German prison sentences, 75% are for under one year, 92% are for under two years, and most of those terms are suspended, compared to an average prison sentence of three years or more in the U.S.[140] In contrast to the way mothers in prison are often separated from their child at birth, Germany allows mothers to parent their children up to age three.[141]

A German prison cell

---

[137] Ram Subramanian and Alison Shames, "Sentencing and Prison Practices in Germany and the Netherlands: Implications for the United States", Vera Institute of Justice, 10/2013.
[138] Turner and Travis, "What We Learned from German Prisons"
[139] Subramanian and Shames, "Sentencing and Prison Practices in Germany and the Netherlands: Implications for the United States".
[140] Ibid.
[141] Ibid.

Germany spends less money per prisoner than Scandinavia does, but it still achieves recidivism rates about half of ours. A major reason for their lower costs is that prisons in Germany are reserved for murderers, rapists and career criminals. While they do have some prisoners who have been involved with gangs and drugs, the number is far smaller than in the U.S. Those with mental illness are sent to psychiatric hospitals rather than to prison.[142]

Even maximum security prisons in Germany emphasize reintegration back into society. Guards are specially trained to calm prisoners down,[143] and the prisoners respond well to that by becoming more peaceable and willing to listen to the guards.

As in Scandinavia, prisoners wear street clothes, not prison uniforms, and many have keys to their own, relatively comfortable rooms.[144]

The Americas

Closer to home, examples in our hemisphere yield some similar lessons. One of the main lessons is that both incarceration rates and violent crime rates are much lower in Canada than for us, more nearly like Western Europe.[145] A key reason is that Canada has a much more peaceable culture, while many countries in the Americas are wracked by drug

---

[142] Subramanian and Shames, "Sentencing and Prison Practices in Germany and the Netherlands: Implications for the United States".
[143] Ibid.
[144] 60 Minutes, 4/13/2016
[145] Roy Walmsley, "World Prison Population List", 11th edition, World Prison Brief, Institute for Criminal Policy Research, Birkbeck University of London, 2016, http://www.prisonstudies.org/sites/default/files/resources/downloads/world_pris on_population_list_11th_edition_0.pdf

wars and violence between gangs fighting each other for this trade.

However, as the statistics comparing these North American neighbors to our north and south show, the murder rates in most countries in the Americas south of the U.S. are much higher than ours,[146] even though their incarceration rates are lower. This is quite different from the lower murder rates in Europe and most other countries.

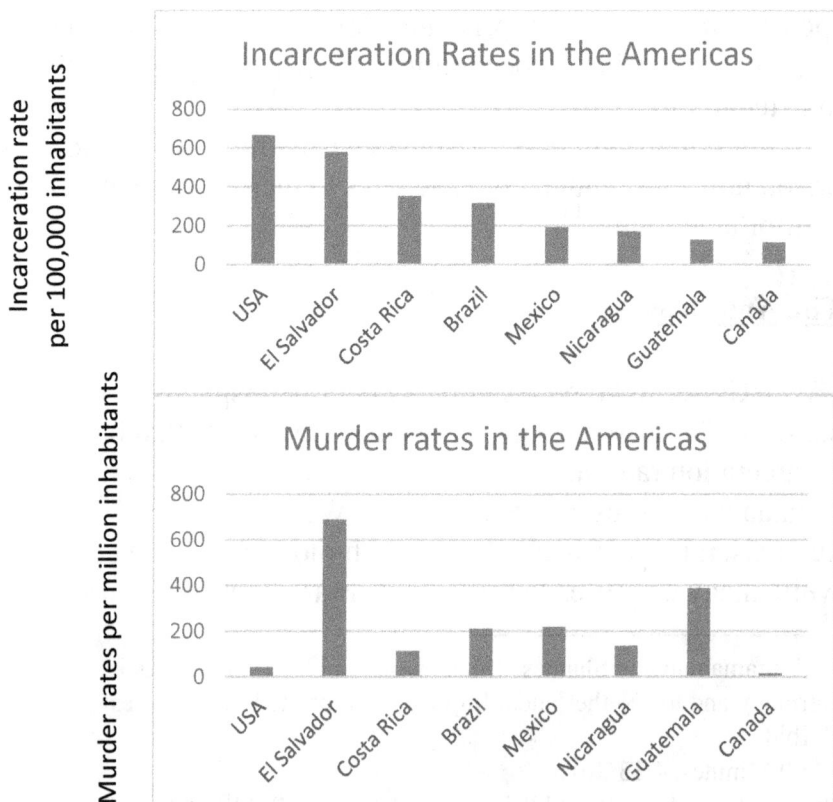

---

[146] NationMaster, "Crime > Violent crime > Murder rate per million people: Countries Compared" http://www.nationmaster.com/country-info/stats/Crime/Violent-crime/Murder-rate-per-million-people

We'll start with our northern neighbor, **Canada**. Canada experiences less than half the violent crime as the U.S.[147] and incarcerates fewer people. Part of the reason may be that there is basically no difference in violent crime rates between large urban centers in Canada and rural areas, in contradistinction to large urban centers in the U.S.[148,149,150,151] Unlike the extent of urban crime associated with black poverty in the U.S., Canada's black population is only about a quarter of that of the U.S., and no city over a half million has more than a 13.5% black population.[152]

Homicide rates in Canada follow a very similar time course to those in the U.S., but Canadian rates remain approximately 3 times lower. Even when a crime wave hit, Canada did not increase incarceration.[153] Violent crime and

---

[147] Maire Gannon, "Crime Comparisons between Canada and the United States," Statistics Canada – Catalogue no. 85-002-XIE, vol. 21, no. 11.

[148] *The Growth of Incarceration in the United States: Exploring Causes and Consequences,* National Academies Press, Chapter 1.

[149] In 1995, violent crime rates in large urban areas were 907 per 100,000 compared to 1046 per 100,000 in rural areas. Tim Leonard, "Crime in Major Metropolitan Areas, 1991-1995," Statistics Canada – Catalogue no. 85-002-XPE, vol. 17, no. 5.

[150] Jocelyn Francisco and Christian Chenier, 'A Comparison Of Large Urban, Small Urban And Rural Crime Rates, 2005", Statistics Canada – Catalogue No. 85-002-XIE, vol. 27, no. 3.

[151] "Crime in the United States 2011," U.S. Department of Justice, Federal Bureau of Investigation, Criminal Justice Information Services Division, Table 16, https://ucr.fbi.gov/crime-in-the-u.s/2011/crime-in-the-u.s.-2011/tables/table_16_rate_number_of_crimes_per_100000_inhabitants_by_population_group_2011.xls

[152] "Demographics of Canada", *Wikipedia*; https://en.wikipedia.org/wiki/Demographics_of_Canada

[153] Barry Latzer, *The Rise and Fall of Violent Crime in America*, 2015, Chapter 5.

incarceration rates have both fallen since 1992.[154,155,156] Violent crime rates similarly declined in Canada, as in the U.S. during this time, though at a lower rate, since Canada never experienced violent crime rates as high as the U.S.[157] Under the circumstances, Canada never felt compelled to impose harsh sentences, with the result that mean and median sentences for violent crimes are very much shorter in Canada[158] than in the U.S.:[159]

---

[154] "Police-reported Crime Statistics in Canada, 2013," Statistics Canada – Catalogue no. 85-002-X, Juristat, May 2014, Table 1b, statcan.gc.ca/pub/85-002-x/2014001/article/14040/tbl/tbl01b-eng.htm

[155] "Incarceration Rates in Canada vs America," http://canadavsamerica.com/incarceration-rates-in-canada-vs-america/

[156] "Uniform Crime Reporting Statistics, estimated violent crime rate", U.S. Department of Justice; https://www.ucrdatatool.gov/Search/Crime/State/RunCrimeTrendsinOneVar.cfm ; "Bureau of Justice Statistics Bulletin Prisoners 1925-81," *U.S. Department of Justice*, https://www.bjs.gov/content/pub/pdf/p2581.pdf; "Prisoners in Custody of State or Federal Correctional Authorities 1977-98, "http://www.bjs.gov/index.cfm?ty=pbdetail&lid=2080 ; "Prisoners in 2000," http://www.bjs.gov/index.cfm?ty=pbdetail&lid=927; "Prisoners in 2005," http://www.bjs.gov/index.cfm?ty=pbdetail&lid=912; "Prisoners in 2015," http://www.bjs.gov/index.cfm?ty=pbdetail&lid=5869

[157] Valerie Pottie Bunge, Holly Johnson and Thierno A. Balde, "Exploring Crime Patterns in Canada", Statistics Canada – Catalogue no. 85-561-MIE, no. 005.

[158] Mikhail Thomas, "Adult Criminal Court Statistics, 2003/04", Statistics Canada – Catalogue no. 85-002-XPE, vol. 24, no. 12.

[159] "Sourcebook of Criminal Justice Statistics," University at Albany, School of Criminal Justice, Hindelang Criminal Justice Research Center, http://www.albany.edu/sourcebook/tost_5.html#5_p

	Mean sentence in months	Median sentence in months
Canadian courts	10	2
U.S. state courts	71	36
U.S. large county courts	94	48
U.S. federal district courts	97	64

This difference could be very significant. Evidently, shorter sentences in Canada have not led to violent crime rates as high as those in the U.S.

There are a few other differences that might suggest ways to reduce the U.S. prison population. In 1999, about 9% of all Canadian cases went to trial, approximately double that in the U.S.[160] Thus, less plea bargaining would help, although that would be expensive. In the 1990's, Canada spent about $20 per citizen for legal aid (public defenders),[161] more than double what we spend.[162] More adequate representation for the indigent would certainly help reduce the number of inappropriate plea deals and reduce the casework overload of U.S. public defenders, and such defense representation would probably be less costly than more trials.

---

[160] Jennifer Pereira and Craig Grimes, "Case Processing in Criminal Courts, 1999/00", Statistics Canada – Catalogue no. 85-002-XIE, vol. 22, no. 1.

[161] Rebecca Johnstone and Jennifer Thomas, "Legal Aid in Canada: 1996-97", Statistics Canada – Catalogue no. 85-002-XIE, vol. 18, no. 10.

[162] Donald J. Farole, Jr., "Bureau of Justice Statistics, A National Assessment of Public Defender Office Caseloads", Justice Research and Statistics Association Annual Meeting, October 28, 2010, www.jrsa.org/events/conferences /presentations-10/Donald_Farole.pdf

The clearance rate for violent crime in Canada is about 72%,[163] much higher than the 46.8% reported in the U.S.[164] More serious police detective work might help reduce crime statistics and take the guilty off the streets.

Restorative justice programs in Canada have been shown to reduce recidivism by almost one-half. These programs require convicts to apologize to their victims, work to provide restitution to their victims, and perform community service. This approach seems to work better with adults than with juveniles.[165]

Unfortunately, it is difficult to prevent violent criminals from carrying guns in the United States. While only 2% of violent crime victims in Canada encounter a gun,[166] even 25% of robberies in the U.S. involved guns.[167] Gun ownership in rural Canada is equally valued as in the rural U.S., but Canadians seem less likely to use their guns in the commission of crimes.

In **Brazil**, education has been used as a way to cut down on both crime and the cost of dealing with convicted criminals. To implement this approach, criminal justice

---

[163] Tina Hotton Mahony and John Turner, "Police-reported clearance rates in Canada, 2010", Statistics Canada – Catalogue no. 85-002-X, Juristat, June, 2012.

[164] "Crime in the United States 2012", FBI: UCR, https://ucr.fbi.gov/crime-in-the-u.s/2012/crime-in-the-u.s.-2012/offenses-known-to-law-enforcement/clearances

[165] "Restorative Justice and Recidivism", Government of Canada, Public Safety Canada, Research Summary, vol 8, no. 1, 1/2003; https://www.publicsafety.gc.ca/cnt/rsrcs/pblctns/jstc-rcdvs/index-en.aspx

[166] Tracey Leesti, "Weapons and Violent Crime", Statistics Canada – Catalogue no. 85-002-XPE, vol. 17, no. 7.

[167] Cook, Philip J. (1987). "Robbery Violence". *Journal of Criminal Law and Criminology*. 70 (2). NCJ 108118.

officials started a low cost rehabilitation program entitled "Rehabilitation through Reading," which encouraged prisoners to wipe four days off their sentences for every preapproved work of literature, philosophy, or science which they read and then wrote a summary about. This proved to be a very inexpensive way to help cope with Brazil's criminal problem, and it is far more humane than all the killings by Brazilian police, who have killed as many people (11,000) in 5 years as police in the U.S. have done in 30.[168]

More strikingly, in 2003 the **Dominican Republic** made literacy compulsory for prisoners in most of their facilities. They also provided prisoners with more educational programs, provided their guards with special training, and assisted ex-cons in finding jobs. Due to these programs, the recidivism rate in the Dominican Republic dropped from 50% to less than 5% wherever those systems were implemented.[169]

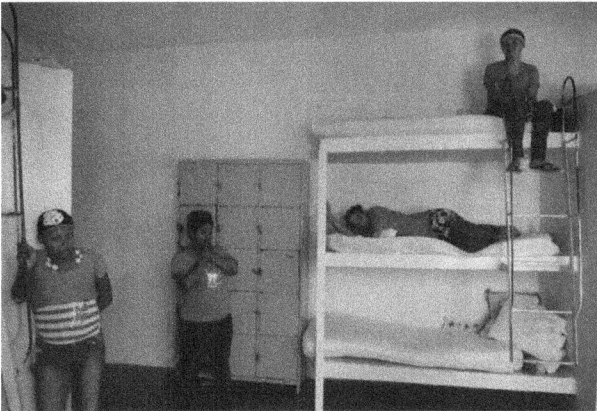

[168] Baz Dreisinger, *Incarceration Nations: A Journey to Justice in Prisons Around the World,* 2016, chapter 5.
[169] Ezra Fieser, "Dominican Republic's More Humane Prison Model", *Reuters World News,* 5/23/2014; https://www.reuters.com/article/us-dominican-prison-reform/dominican-republics-more-humane-prison-model-idUSBREA4M0GW20140523

Africa and Asia

Prisons in other countries have cut down their costs of incarceration by using reconciliation and offsite work as a form of restitution. Though these are approaches described by liberal prison reform advocates such as Baz Dreisinger,[170] these approaches do offer useful lessons for conservatives because of the financial savings. Here are some examples of how these programs were implemented in countries in Africa and Asia.

Rwanda, site of the horrific genocide between Hutsis and Tutus, has emphasized forgiveness in order to promote reconciliation, despite the lingering anger between the two sides. Almost half of the people who would normally be in

---

[170] Dreisinger, *Incarceration Nations,* 2016

prison perform work travelling to different regions of the country to make up for their crimes. Those that are in prison can go on work leave, and, as in Norway, play sports like soccer with their guards. They get to keep 10% of their pay (far more than in the U.S.), and they have prisoner-run government for their prisons.[171]

South Africa similarly emphasizes reconciliation by providing restorative justice between criminals and their victims.[172] This means that criminals have to pay their victims an agreed upon amount, as determined by the court, to make up for their crime.

In Asia, Australia incarcerates a higher percentage of aboriginals than we do blacks in the U.S. As in Africa, Australia has prisoners work offsite to provide reparations to the community. In addition, Australia has humane private prisons which help to prepare their "residents" for release in private pre-release centers.[173] The "residents" go to school and farm on-site or work off-site providing reparations to the outside community, where they also go to alcoholics anonymous and narcotics anonymous meetings. Female residents get to see their children regularly. The private prisons are run by a Serco, a company with a $10 billion dollar portfolio, a staff of 100,000 and contracts in 30 countries. Their contracts include recidivism-based measures as incentives. Thus private prisons can be very humane and even save money over their government-run counterparts.

---

[171] Dreisinger, *Incarceration Nations*, 2016, Chapter 1.
[172] Ibid., Chapter 2.
[173] Ibid., Chapter 6.

Singapore managed to reduce its recidivism rate from 40% in 2000 down to 23.6% in 2010 by helping convicts leaving prison find jobs. Even though Singapore effectively excludes most of its ex-cons from better jobs, their inmates enjoy a staggering 99% success rate in finding jobs in the food, beverage, retail, or tourism industries. Prisoners do most of the baking for their airlines and laundry for their hospitals, though they are not given any additional education to prepare them for these jobs. But the prison provides help in finding the jobs and provides the needed training. Singapore emphasizes punishment much more than in Europe, such as by making inmates sleep on straw mats and keeping them locked up in cells 23 hours a day for the first tenth of their sentences. However, the prisons prepare their convicts for release by requiring them to participate in three rehabilitation phases:

1) They have to work together in teams with individuals from different ethnicities, so they learn to work together with those from other ethnic groups;

2) They have to renounce their participation in gangs;

3) Then, the prison prepares them with skills and jobs for their release.[174]

Summing Up

Although the methods of defining and counting recidivism vary from country to country, making comparison difficult,[175] we can still learn from other countries many

---

[174] Dreisinger, *Incarceration Nations*, Chapter 7.
[175] Seena Fazel and Achim Wolf, "A Systematic Review of Criminal Recidivism Rates Worldwide: Current Difficulties and Recommendations for Best Practices", *Plos One* 6/18/2015; journals.plos.org/plosone/article?id=10.1371/journal.pone.0130390

ways to improve prison practices here. In summary, prison policies in other countries suggest that:

- ❖ **observations**
- ➢ **recommendations**

- ❖ When properly implemented, treating prisoners with more respect and humanity succeeds in getting them to take responsibility for their actions instead of blaming "the system" that incarcerated them.

- ❖ An emphasis on rehabilitation helps more than the current U.S. emphasis on punishment. The focus on rehabilitation reduces recidivism and results in a calmer, more peaceful prison environment, so inmates are less likely to cause trouble, such as through fights or riots.

- ❖ When properly implemented, an emphasis on rehabilitation can result in shorter sentences, less recidivism, and considerable savings.

  - ➢ We should increase the emphasis on rehabilitation as opposed to punishment.

- ❖ Shorter sentence lengths can reduce over-incarceration.

- ❖ Hiring more public defenders to prevent inappropriate plea deals would also reduce incarceration.

- ❖ Solving crimes at a higher clearance rate with more detectives might help reduce crime.

➢ We should reduce sentence lengths and hire more public defenders and police detectives.

❖ Establishing restorative justice practices based on restitution would allow criminals to compensate their victims outside of prison or jail.

➢ The majority of prisoner wages should be used to make restitution to their victims.

➢ Prisoners should be instructed in a trade in order to make them much more employable upon release.

❖ Fostering different ethnicities working together on teams in rehabilitation programs would help prisoners have a more successful re-entry into society.

❖ Providing assistance to increase literacy reduces recidivism.

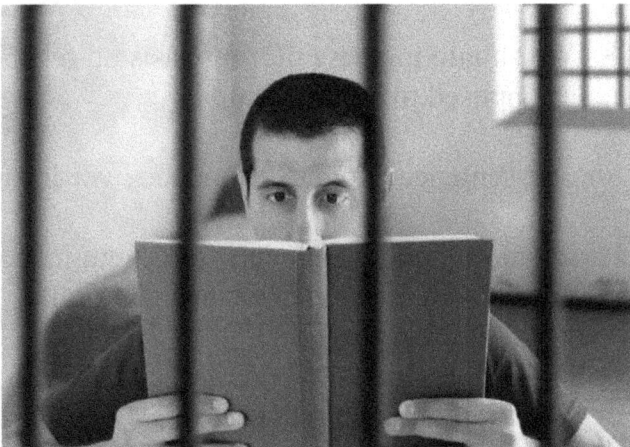

CHAPTER 4 – HOW OREGON AND NEW YORK CITY HAVE DEALT WITH PRISONS AND RECIDIVISM

States vary widely in both their choices regarding incarceration and their calculations of recidivism rates, as reflected in a 2011 study by the Pew Center.[176] The study not only equated recidivism as "the revolving door of America's prisons," but found a wide variation in rates, ranging from states with 3-year recidivism rates as low as 22.8% to other states with rates as high as 65.8%. Some of this disparity is due to the fact that states interpret and calculate recidivism differently. Some states count rearrests (a high number), some include a former prisoner's return to prison for both new arrests and technical violations of parole (an intermediate number), and some count imprisonment due only to a new crime (a low number).

These factors complicate comparisons, but they help to illustrate the high financial costs of recidivism and over-incarcerating individuals for less serious, non-violent crimes.

The following chapter will illustrate the different ways that Oregon and New York City have affected recidivism rates by their prison policies.

Oregon

The Pew Center study concluded that Oregon was a standout compared to other states in reducing recidivism by

---

[176]Pew Center, "State of Recidivism, The Revolving Door of America's Prisons," 2011. http://www.pewtrusts.org/en/research-and-analysis/reports/0001/01/01/state-of-recidivism

its more prisoner-supportive policies coupled with fair but firm sanctions for parole violations. The Oregon recidivism rate was 22.8% from 2004 to 2007. A reason for their lower recidivism rate compared to other states is that Oregon inmates receive an initial assessment of risk and need, along with 6 months of transition planning leading to their release. After release, prisoners remain on parole during re-entry.

Estimates for the number of released prisoners returned to prison for technical violations of parole range from 33% to 50%.[177,178,179] These numbers could definitely be reduced so as to decrease incarceration for such minor lapses (and thus incarceration overall). Technical violations of parole can involve failure to pay court-imposed fees by parolees or failure to pass a drug test. Perhaps the biggest change Oregon instituted was that it virtually eliminated sending technical parole violators back to prison, since they had only committed a technical violation of their parole conditions rather than committing a new crime. Instead, the Oregon parole system generated a graduated series of sanctions for parole violations, including a fine or a short jail stay to hold parole violators accountable. But a return to prison was considered the last possible option.

---

[177] Lois M. Davis, Robert Bozick, Jennifer Steele, Jessica Saunders and Jeremy Miles,"Education and Vocational Training in Prisons Reduces Recidivism, Improves Job Outlook", RAND, News Release 8/22/2013, http://www.rand.org/news/press/2013/08/22.html

[178] "Evidence Based Practice to Reduce Recidivision," Crime and Justice Institute, 2012. http://www.nationaltasc.org/wp-content/uploads/2012/11/Evidence-Based-Practice-to-Reduce-Recidivism-Crime-and-Justice-Institute-NIC.pdf

[179] John Pfaff, *Locked In*, 2017, pp 39-40. While I believe Pfaff is correct in nearly all his analysis of the criminal justice system, I believe he has underestimated the influence terminating imprisonment for technical violations of parole might have.

While some may argue that Oregon's approach to dealing with prisoners just transfers the burden from the prison to parole, the costs of parole are several times lower than those of prison. Moreover, the parole environment is more humane and requires parolees to exercise more responsibility than prisoners are normally allowed in prison.

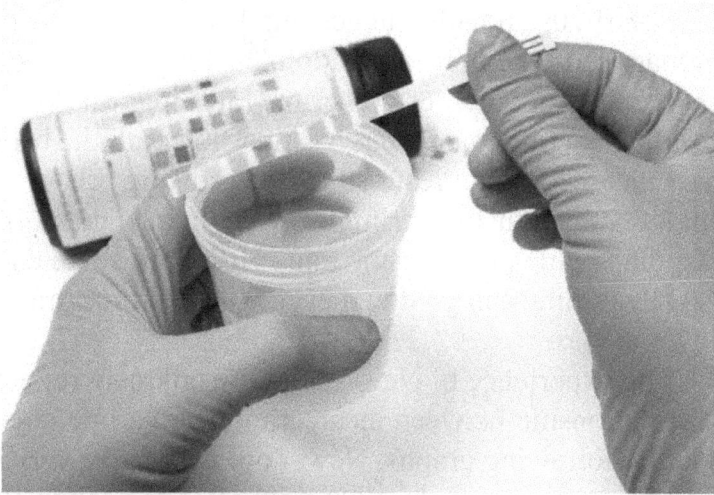

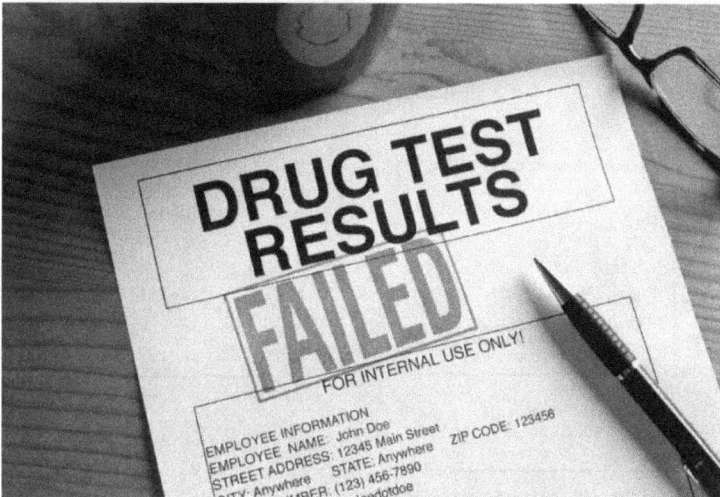

New York City: Does It Offer Tips to Reduce Incarceration Without Increasing Crime?

Incarceration rates and crime rates sometimes change in tandem (correlate), but often they do not, as described in the discussion in Chapter 1 about the nationwide relationship between crime and punishment. To recapitulate, both rates rose in the 1970s and 80s, suggesting that crime drove a reactionary increase in incarceration.[180] However, as the prison population grew further, crime rates in the 1990s declined,[181] leading many conservatives to extoll the benefits of mass incarceration. Presumably, the growing prison population meant that the criminals were being taken off the streets, thus reducing the crime rate. However, some data suggest that crime can go down even when incarceration rates go down.

The experience of New York City uniquely reflects such a relationship between incarceration and crime rates. As seen in the following graphs, New York City had a very high violent crime rate that reduced rapidly after its peak in 1991, and incarceration actually declined over most of that time, unlike incarceration in the country as a whole.

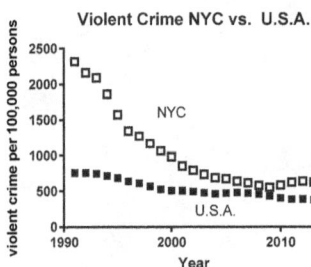

_____

[180] Enns, *Incarceration Nation,* 2016.
[181] Pfaff, *Locked In,* 2017, p. 4.

Many books have been written about how New York reduced its crime rate, but none really have analyzed how New York reduced its incarceration rate at the same time.

Major Factor 1 in Reducing Violent Crime in NYC: Reducing Recidivism

Franklin Zimring found that the major factor contributing to the cause of decreased crime in New York City was the city's ability to reduce recidivism. Since the homicide rate was down, and so was incarceration, Zimring asked where all the criminals had gone. That's when he found that recidivism, as measured by the formerly incarcerated committing new felonies, dropped sharply after 1990, and that's what led him to suggest that reducing recidivism is a key to reducing crime.[182,183]

Unfortunately, it was not clear to Zimring how career criminals were dissuaded from committing new felonies. Curiously, New York accomplished this by substituting increasing incarceration of those who perpetrated technical violations of parole, thus limiting any decrease in total incarcerations. Imagine how much incarceration would have

---

[182] Franklin E. Zimring, *The City That Became Safe: New York's Lessons for Urban Crime and Its Control*, Oxford University Press, 2012.

[183] Zimring came to this conclusion by eliminating a number of other potential contributions to the decrease in crime. The factors he ruled out included the effect of a large urban environment, demographic changes in racial or ethnic composition, and changes in unemployment, youth employment, poverty, and the proportion of single parent households, and drug use. He also found only minor contributions from misdemeanor marijuana arrests and stop and frisk policing, both of which increased markedly over this time frame. The contributions of these factors are summarized in Appendix III.

declined, if they had restricted incarcerations for technical violations of parole at the same time!

I have analyzed this effect on recidivism further with some New York City data[184] from 1991 to 2011. Recidivism is indicated by the % of releases returned within 3 years for new felonies.

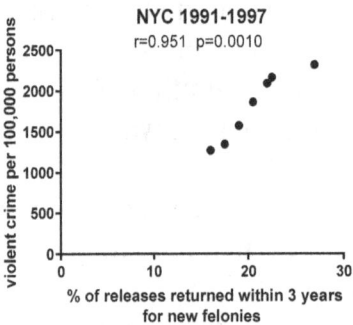

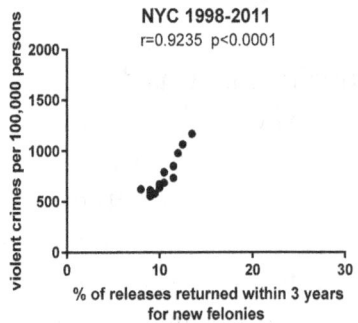

NYC 1991-1997
r=0.951 p=0.0010

NYC 1998-2011
r=0.9235 p<0.0001

In both charts above, the points at upper right occurred early in the time period and those at lower left in the later years. As the above charts show, during this period, New York City experienced a dramatic decline of recidivism associated with new felonies by released prisoners. These declined from 27% of the felons returning to prison within three years, indicated by the high point at upper right of the left chart in 1991 to only 9% returning, indicated by the dots at lower left of the right chart. At the same time, the number of violent crimes per 100,000 crimes went down, so the lower the percent of returns, the lower the number of violent crimes.

---

[184] "New York State Corrections and Community Supervision, 2011" Inmate Releases, Three Year Post-Release Follow-Up, Table 11, www.docs.nygov/Research/Reports/2016/2011_releases_3yr_out.pdf

Thus, from the charts above, it should be clear that less returns to prison within 3 years of release (a measure of recidivism) went hand in hand with a reduction in violent crime.[185] Because the data only shows a correlation -- not one thing causing another -- it is uncertain whether the reduction in crime led to reducing recidivism or whether the reduction in recidivism led to a reduction in violent crime. However, there is a strong possibility that reduced recidivism contributed to the reduced violent crime in New York City and thus taxpayer savings.

How was this reduction in recidivism related to changes in incarceration? Was it associated with reduced incarceration? From 1991 to 1997, when incarceration was still increasing slightly, significant decreases in recidivism occurred without much change in incarceration. However, the New York City data from 1998 to 2011 suggests reduced recidivism went hand in hand with overall reduced incarceration, and it may even have been responsible for much of the reduced incarceration.

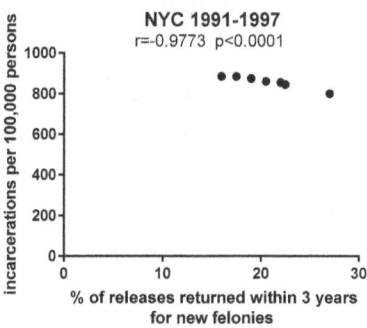

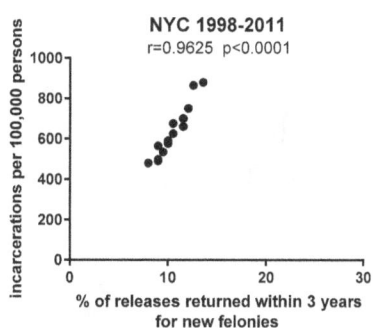

---

[185] The average recidivism rate over these years was a modest 42%, below the national average.

As the chart on the right illustrates, at the same time that the number of incarcerations per 100,000 prisoners went down, so did the percent of ex-convicts who came back to prison for new felonies.

Thus, from 1998 to 2011, the reduction in recidivism due to new felonies could very well be responsible for the reductions in **both** violent crime and incarceration. These findings suggest that New York City's ability to reduce recidivism over that period may have been the key to its ability to reduce incarceration without increasing violent crime.

The reduction in overall recidivism was less than it might have been because an increasing number of the returning prisoners were sent back due to technical parole violations. Accordingly, during the entire period from 1991 to 2011, the total returns of released prisoners was down only a small amount -- from about 45% to 35%. Many criminologists have been advocating a decrease in reimprisonment for technical violations of parole.[186] Eliminating technical violations of parole would likely lead to an even greater decrease in incarceration, resulting in more savings to the local community and the economy generally, and it would be unlikely to result in increases in violent crime.

---

[186] Witness the discussion of recidivism in Oregon on pages 98-99.

Major Factor 2 in Reducing Violent Crime in NYC: Increased Incarceration

Small increases in incarceration were correlated with strong reductions in violent crime in New York City during the period 1991 to 1997,[187] as seen below left. However, after 1998, the right hand panel shows that incarceration and violent crime both decreased from upper right to lower left, providing a very strong correlation.

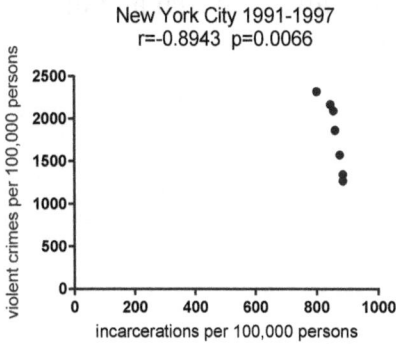

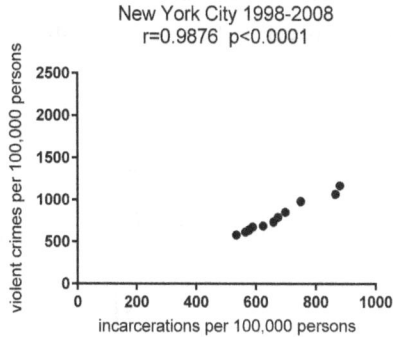

New York City 1991-1997
r=-0.8943 p=0.0066

New York City 1998-2008
r=0.9876 p<0.0001

On the left it is difficult to imagine how reduced crime would lead to increased incarceration. If anything, the increased incarceration led to the decreased crime.

On the right, it is difficult to imagine how reduced incarceration would lead to reduced violent crime. More likely, reduced crime led to reduced incarceration.

So what led to the decreases in violent crime from 1998 onward? Could incarceration in jails have been involved?

---

[187] as seen nationally from 1993 to 2005 in Chapter 1.

How Did Incarcerating Convicts in Jail Affect Crime Rates?

What about the effect of incarceration in New York City jails? To what extent did increased incarceration in jail affect the crime rate?

It would seem that increasing the number of inmates with determinate sentences of up to a year -- the longest time that an inmate can be held in a jail rather than be assigned to a prison -- has reduced violent crime.[188] From 2001 to 2009, the proportion of inmates serving time grew from 14% to 49%, with fewer inmates being held in jail awaiting trial and more sentenced to jail for a violent felony:[189]

New York City 2001-2009
r=-0.9909 p<0.0001

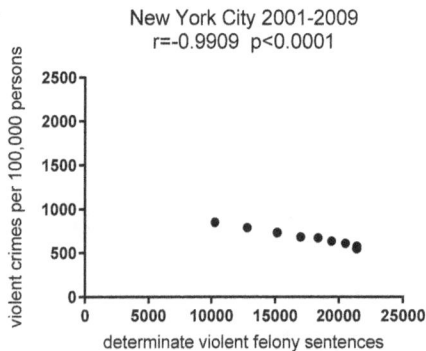

Thus, at a time when there was less prison incarceration to decrease violent crime, as shown on the previous page, increased jail incarceration might have been a

---

[188] It is unlikely that reduced violent crime resulted in more jail inmates for violent felonies.

[189] "Under Custody Report: Profile of Inmate Population Under Custody on January 1, 2013," State of New York Department of Corrections and Community Supervision, Table 17B.

factor in the reduction of violent crime, although as previously discussed, many other factors could have led to fewer violent crimes. Incarceration in jails involved shorter sentences than those in prison, resulting in less incarceration overall.

Thus, it is very likely that modest increases in incarceration in prisons reduced violent crime from 1991 to 1997, and greater incarceration in jails continued the reduction in violent crime from 2001 to 2009.

Interestingly, increases in the jailed population were no longer important for crime reduction after 2012. Between 2012 and 2016, the % of arrests that resulted in jail terms declined from 13.2% to 10.7%, while the reductions in prison terms (8.4% to 7.9%) or probation (4.5% to 4.2%) were much less.[190]

Major Factor 3 in Reducing Violent Crime in NYC: Increased Police Staffing

Police staffing experienced an uptick, particularly when the decline in homicides was greatest, perhaps because the increased police presence discouraged potential killers. Zimring noted that increased police targeting of crime hot spots and of open air drug markets could not be ruled out as potential factors contributing to the decline in homicide, though their influence was hard to quantify. This targeting may have discouraged potential homicides.

---

[190] "New York City Adult Arrests Disposed, 2012-2016", New York State Division of Criminal Justice Services; http://www.criminaljustice.ny.gov/crimnet/ojsa/dispos/nyc.pdf

By the same token, Zimring found the police use of Compstat mapping, information and planning systems was a probable contributor, perhaps because the police used these systems to better target crime hot spots. Thus, Zimring surmised that police staffing and other police policies were greater contributors to reducing homicide than increased misdemeanor marijuana arrests and stop and frisk stops.

Zimring considered police staffing a significant factor, finding a correlation between more staffing and less violent crime. I find the same result as indicated on the chart below:

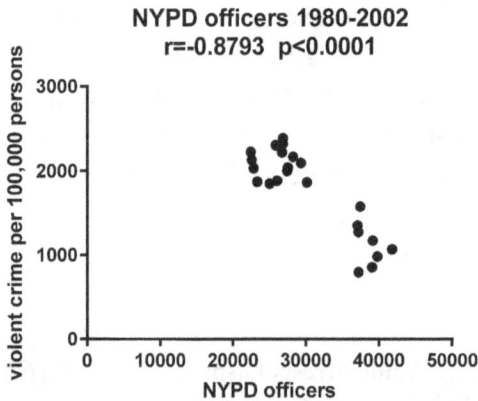

NYPD officers 1980-2002
r=-0.8793 p<0.0001

This increase in police staffing may have resulted in more incarcerations, but the mere presence of more police with improved tactics might also have contributed to the decline in violent crime.

Other Contributing Factors in Reducing Violent Crime in NYC

Zimring concluded that approximately half of the New York City crime decline was not due to any particular cause. He may have overlooked the national crime decline, which was about half that of New York City's. In fact, the New York City homicide rate in 2007 had declined to almost exactly that of the U.S. average. So maybe some larger social or economic factors affecting the U.S. economy as a whole had some influence. For example, prior to the Great Recession that started in 2008, the economy seemed to be booming, and consumer confidence was high. So maybe the generally positive national mood contributed to people feeling less stress, and therefore they were less likely to strike out by deadly attacks on others.

It is more difficult to assess the contributory effects of certain specific programs, but these are likely to be more than minor contributors to the simultaneous decrease of crime and incarceration in New York City. One program, SHOCK, graduated over 50,000 inmates with high school equivalent GED degrees, and it is estimated to have saved taxpayers close to $1.5 billion since its inception about 30 years ago. Another program is the Drug Treatment Alternative-to-Prison program (DTAP), whose participants were 36% less likely to be reconvicted and 67% less likely to return to prison.[191]

Minor Factors in Reducing Violent Crime in NYC

It has been more difficult to credit a particular policy for the decrease in New York City homicide, violent crime, or crime generally. Particularly after 1997, when incarceration was going down, there were claims in favor of major contributions of many factors in crime reduction, such as the stop-and-frisk and broken windows policies, more strategic policing, using CompStat to target crime hot spots, increased drug arrests, decreased parole release, and decreased lead toxicity. I determined that the contributions of stop-and-frisk and broken windows were more minor and discuss them together with decreased lead toxicity in Appendix III.

Then, too, individuals were eager to claim credit: mayors Giuliani (1994-2001) and Bloomberg (2002-2015), police commissioners Kelly (1992-1994), Bratton (1994-1996), Safir (1996-2000), Kerik (2000-2001), Kelly (2002-2013), and Bratton (2014-2016).[192]

In short, there seem to be a large number of factors associated with a decrease in crime, arrests, convictions, and incarceration in some way, making it hard to know what really are the most influential causal factors.

---

[191] Dareh Gregorian, " NYC Jail, Prison Incarceration Rates Drop by Over 50 Percent as Crime Falls", *New York Daily News*, 10/28/2016. http://www.nydailynews.com/new-york/nyc-jail-prison-incarceration-rates-drop-50-crime-falls-article-1.2848822

[192] Ellen Belcher, "NYPD-Historical and Current Research: Police Commissioners", Lloyd Sealy Library, John Jay College of Criminal Justice, http://guides.lib.jjay.cuny.edu/c.php?g=288325&p=1922504

The tenure of individual police commissioners was too short to adequately analyze, so we'll only discuss mayors. Crime went down much more for Giuliani than for Bloomberg, but incarceration went down much more for Bloomberg than for Giuliani. This suggests that Giuliani's get-tough policies may have been more effective, but only by increasing incarceration. Policies under Bloomberg probably succeeded better at keeping crime low while decreasing incarceration.

Lessons to Be Drawn from NYC

So what policies might have reduced crime, especially without increasing incarceration? Certainly, some policies have had more effect than others in New York City. However, complicating matters is the fact that a policy may be effective during one time period, but then it may become less effective for any number of reasons.

Then, too, policies that may have an impact in one city may not in another due to differing conditions in different cities. For example, while New York City policies may be more relevant for urban crime in other large cities, it is not possible to know whether or not those policies will be effective at a different time in other large cities which may have different local problems.

Still, some of the policies that worked in New York City to reduce both crime and incarceration should be among the first to be tried in other cities. Thus, some policies to try out first might be:

> reduce recidivism, particularly by reducing imprisonment for technical violators of parole,

- increase imprisonment when violent crime is very high,

- put more felons in jail rather than prison,

- increase the number of police officers assigned to a targeted high crime area.

More Incarceration Does Not Always Result in Less Crime

Aside from New York City, New Jersey, Texas and California all reduced their prison populations over 20% between 1999 and 2012, while crime in all three states fell faster than the national average.[193] These observations undermine the fear that releasing some prisoners to the community will increase the crime rate due to "dangerous" prisoners back on the streets.

In turn, the authors of "The Growth of Incarceration in the United States: Exploring Causes and Consequence" conclude that the increase in incarceration probably had little to do with the decrease or deterrence of crime. As they remarked in their conclusions:

> "CONCLUSION: The increase in incarceration may have caused a decrease in crime, but the magnitude of the reduction is highly uncertain and the results of most studies suggest it was unlikely to have been large."

---

[193] James Austin, Lauren-Brooke Eisen with James Cullen and Jonathan Frank, "How Many Americans are Unnecessarily Incarcerated?", Brennan Center for Justice, Twenty Years,2016; https://www.brennancenter.org/sites/default/files/publications/Unnecessarily_Incarcerated.pdf

"CONCLUSION: The incremental deterrent effect of increases in lengthy prison sentences is modest at best. Because recidivism rates decline markedly with age, lengthy prison sentences, unless they specifically target very high-rate or extremely dangerous offenders, are an inefficient approach to preventing crime by incapacitation."

"CONCLUSION: The change in penal policy over the past four decades may have had a wide range of unwanted social costs, and the magnitude of crime reduction benefits is highly uncertain."[194]

A correlation analysis I performed shows a moderately strong correlation between incarceration rates and violent crime rates when comparing these two rates in 2010 across the 50 states and Washington, D.C.[195,196] I believe this correlation indicates that it is likely that more crime leads to more incarceration (or that less crime results in less incarceration). This relationship is reflected in the chart below, which shows the number of violent crimes per 100,000 people and the prison and jail rate, which clearly goes up as the number of violent crimes increase. Alternatively, as posited on page 27, increased incarceration might act as a school for criminals, leading to increased crime.

---

[194] Jeremy Travis, Bruce Western and Steve Redburn, Editors, *The Growth of Incarceration in the United States: Exploring Causes and Consequences,* National Academies Press, 2014, pp. 4, 5, 7.

[195] 2010 Census data; http://www.ojp.doj.gov/bjs/correct.htm

[196] The top right data point represents Washington, D.C. If it is left out, the r value becomes 0.5374, and the p value remains <0.0001. Thus, even though Washington, D.C. is an outlier due to its high crime in a highly urban area, the correlation still holds for all 50 states.

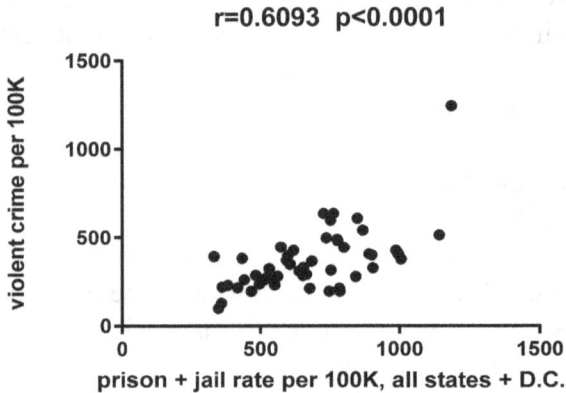

r=0.6093 p<0.0001

violent crime per 100K (y-axis)

prison + jail rate per 100K, all states + D.C. (x-axis)

While a correlation in and of itself does not generally indicate causation,[194] this relationship between violent crime and the prison and jail rate just might. Not only does it suggest that more crime results in more incarceration, but it also suggests that more incarceration is unlikely to cause a significant decrease in violent crime, because in that case the points should decline toward the right of the chart instead of increasing.

Conclusions

One lesson to be learned from comparisons of prison policy between states, as with comparisons between countries discussed in the previous chapter, is that rehabilitation can be used to reduce recidivism. However, the degree of success depends on a number of factors. These include a supportive environment from guards and other prisoners, a willingness of the prisoner to change, and an openness of local company employers to be receptive to providing a job to a prisoner on

---

[194] Other factors could contribute to the correlation and thus negate causality.

probation, parole, or just released from prison, as will be discussed further in the next chapter.

We have seen that Oregon and New York City both managed to reduce incarceration by reducing recidivism. Oregon did so by reducing imprisonment for technical violations of parole, whereas New York City reduced recidivism by reducing the commitment of new felonies by ex-offenders. Imagine what could happen if both effects could be effected somewhere at the same time. Or if that somewhere could be nationwide...

In summary, policy in different states suggests the following:

- ❖ **observations**
- ➤ **recommendations**

- ❖ When properly implemented, an emphasis on rehabilitation can result in shorter sentences, less recidivism, and considerable savings.

- ❖ Reducing the likelihood of jail or prison time for petty offenses or technical violations of parole or probation reduces both recidivism and costs.

  - ➤ Reduce recidivism, starting by reducing imprisonment for technical violators of parole or probation.

  - ➤ Further reduce recidivism by following up on New York City's accomplishment of reducing the commitment of new felonies by ex-offenders on parole.

- ❖ It is possible to reduce violent crime at the same time that incarceration is reduced.

  - ➤ Increase imprisonment only when violent crime is very high,

  - ➤ Put more felons in jail rather than prison. This can be accomplished by reducing sentence length to less than a year for certain crimes.

- ❖ In urban settings, more police officers on the beat may act as another deterrent to crime, even if the police don't make additional stops or arrests.

  - ➤ Increase the number of police officers assigned to a targeted high crime area.

Among these actions, reducing recidivism is key and constitutes the subject of the next chapter.

CHAPTER 5 – REDUCING RECIDIVISM

Reducing recidivism is a key way to both reduce crime and costs, so any strategies to reduce recidivism, even if more costly in the near term, can be much more cost effective in the long term.

One key to achieving less recidivism is helping ex-cons adjust to life outside prison. President George W. Bush pointed this out in his 2004 State of the Union Address, when he spoke about the difficulty that ex-cons have in adjusting to life outside of prison, resulting in a high rate of recidivism. As he stated:

> "This year, some 600,000 inmates will be released from prison back into society. We know from long experience that if they can't find work, or a home, or help, they are much more likely to commit more crimes and return to prison.... America is the land of the second chance, and when the gates of the prison open, the path ahead should lead to a better life."[198]

But unfortunately, the path ahead does not usually lead to this better life; instead the ex-con is confronted with difficult barriers to remaining out of prison at every turn. A key reason for this difficulty is the kind of mental transformation that a prisoner experiences when placed in confinement, and the longer the prison term, the more the prisoner experiences this negative impact on his thinking and identity.

---

[198] President George W. Bush, 2004 State of the Union Address

Former NYPD Commissioner Bernard Kerik stated this dilemma well when he observed that: "Taking away someone's freedom is mind altering. Your objective should not be to treat these individuals like animals but to prepare them for reintegration into society."[199] He should know, because he's been on both sides of the bars, having served as NYPD Commissioner, but then he pleaded guilty to filing false tax returns and lying to the White House, for which he was imprisoned.

Doing something about recidivism now is extremely important, because recidivism in the U.S. is very high and increasing -- and incarceration and associated costs cannot be reduced long term unless the recidivism rates go down. The alarming increase in recidivism is shown by a recent study on Minnesota prisoners, which determined that the average offender in 1981 had 1 prior felony conviction, whereas similar offenders in 1991 had 2, and ones in 2013 had 2.5 felony convictions.[200] Clearly, ex-convicts are re-offending at a rapidly increasing rate that can and must be reversed.

Reducing recidivism is critical, because it is one of the keys to reducing our mass incarceration dilemma. Almost half of those entering prison are ex-cons. A 2007 Department of Justice report concluded that incarceration actually increases offender recidivism.[201] Most prisoners who are released wind up arrested and back in prison, because they are ill prepared to deal with the outside world. According to

---

[199] Kerik, *From Jailer to Jailed,* p. 51.

[200] Ryan King, "Prison Growth," *Ohio State University News*, August 22, 2016, https://news.osu.edu/news/2016/08/22/prison-growth

[201] "Evidence Based Practice to Reduce Recidivision," Crime and Justice Institute, 2012. http://www.nationaltasc.org/wp-content/uploads/2012/11/Evidence-Based-Practice-to-Reduce-Recidivism-Crime-and-Justice-Institute-NIC.pdf

Bureau of Justice statistics, the re-arrest rate for prisoners released in 30 states in 2005 was 57% within one year, 68% within three years, and 77% for the first five years following release.[202] Statistics show that the first year is when the most recidivism occurs, so this is when intervention is most needed to help the ex-con have a successful re-entry. The first year is the time when a newly released convict faces the most difficulty in adjusting to the world outside prison, which can include finding a job, reconnecting with family members, and learning about new changes in technology and society that require adjustment. If the ex-con is able to successfully navigate these new experiences on leaving prison in this first critical year, he or she will be more likely to continue to find success in this new environment, so recidivism later on becomes less likely. But if the ex-con is unable to find the needed assistance or land a job in that critical first year, that can set him or her on the path to reconnecting with old criminal buddies or committing crimes again to get the money to survive.

Still another reason for the high rate of recidivism that must be addressed are technical violations of parole, which account for approximately one-third of the returns to prison,[203] as John Pfaff concluded in *Locked In,* based on conducting dozens of interviews with recidivists.[204] Many

---

[202] The numbers here are higher than those in the Pew Center study referred to in Chapter 4 because they represent rearrest rates, which represents the highest estimate for recidivism.

[203] "Evidence Based Practice to Reduce Recidivism," Crime and Justice Institute, 2012. http://www.nationaltasc.org/wp-content/uploads/2012/11/Evidence-Based-Practice-to-Reduce-Recidivism-Crime-and-Justice-Institute-NIC.pdf

[204] John Pfaff, *Locked In*, 2017, pp 39-40. While I believe Pfaff is correct in nearly all his analysis of the criminal justice system, I believe he has

technical violations can be quite innocuous activities, such as forgetting to contact a parole or probation officer or not having access to a phone to make a check-in call. Other violations might be a prohibited meeting with an old girlfriend who drops by the house or going to a local baseball game where former gang members are present, even though the ex-con has no personal contact with them. Parole and probation officers may take a hard line on such infractions, so rather than give an ex-con a warning, fine, or another chance to stick to the rules in the future, the ex-con may simply be sent back to the slammer. No second chance can mean being incarcerated for an even longer time due to the violation, and an even greater likelihood of recidivism when the prisoner gets out the second time around.

The Effects of Incarceration and Recidivism on Families

Were these difficulties just affecting the convicts, the situation would be bad enough, but their families are impacted, too. As Ross and Richards point out in *Beyond Bars*: "The destruction of the traditional American family is both part of the cause, and in part the result, of the dramatic increase in prison population."[205]

Blacks are disproportionately imprisoned in both prisons and jails, as shown in the following table and incarceration bar growth chart. Consequently, mass incarceration has a very negative effect on black families,

---

underestimated the influence terminating imprisonment for technical violations of parole might have.

[205]Jeffrey Ian Ross and Stephen C. Richards, *Beyond Bars, Rejoining Society after Prison, Alpha, 2009,* p. 109.

particularly in areas of high unemployment among black youths.[206] As this table and chart show very dramatically, though blacks represent only about a third of all prisoners, they are about 3 times as likely to be imprisoned compared to all prisoners. And their rate of imprisonment is even higher when compared to whites -- over 6 times as likely, and they are about 2½ times as likely as Hispanics to be imprisoned.

	All	Whites	Hispanics	Blacks
Imprisoned	1,516,879	505,600	332,200	549,100
Rate of male imprisonment[207]	904	466	1134	2805

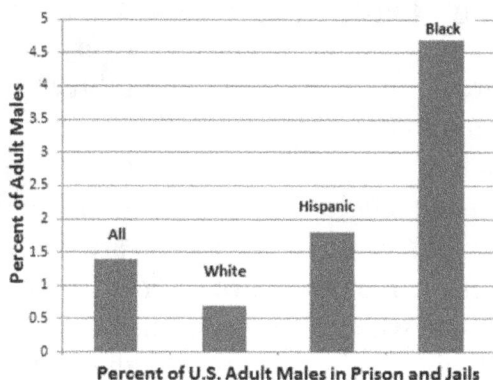

Percent of U.S. Adult Males in Prison and Jails

Blacks are more likely to be imprisoned than other groups because they are more likely to be involved in crimes.

---

[206] Heather C. West, "Statistical Tables, Prison Inmates at Midyear 2009". U.S. Department of Justice, Bureau of Justice Statistics, NCJ 230113, https://www.bjs.gov/content/pub/pdf/pim09st.pdf
[207] Rate = Imprisonments per 100,000 males; E. Ann Carson, "Prisoners in 2013", U.S. Department of Justice Bulletin, 9/30/14, NCJ 247282, Table 8, https://bjs.gov/content/pub/pdf/p13.pdf

When black youths find no jobs, they resort to selling drugs and crime to support themselves.[208] A study of arrests in Chicago indicated that only 25% of the individuals arrested had been employed in the previous four years prior to arrest.[209] Moreover, given this high rate of imprisonment, the high crime and unemployment rate in the neighborhoods they return to, and the difficulty of all prisoners to successfully readjust to re-entry, it is not surprising that blacks have a high rate of recidivism upon release.

In the high crime areas of Washington, D.C., incarceration has increased the ratio of women to men to 60/40, with women resorting to more risky sexual behavior and men having more women partners,[210] hardly conducive to marital harmony. Furthermore, nationwide incarceration and the social response to it has resulted in a very high proportion of black children – more than two out of three[211] -- raised by single moms and in the dissolution of the social fabric of the black community.

These many single women raising their children are less able to get jobs when their children are young, since they have to care for them on their own. Some women may have parents or siblings who can provide some care, but often their parents or siblings are single women with children, too. As

---

[208] Pfaff, *Locked In,* 2017, p. 48.

[209] Charles E. Loeffler (2013) "Pre-imprisonment Employment Drops: Another Instance of the Ashenfelter Dip?", Working paper, referenced in Wendy Still, Barbara Broderick and Steven Raphael, "Building Trust and Legitimacy Within Community Corrections", New Thinking in Community Corrections Bulletin, Washington, D.C.: U.S. Department of Justice, National Institute of Justice, 2016, NCJ 249946.

[210] Pfaff, "Locked In", 2017, p. 122.

[211] "Births to Unmarried Women", Child Trends/Databank Indicator; www.childtrends.org/indicators/births-to-unmarried-women

their children get older, their teenage children are more likely to join gangs, and lacking an adult male parent to serve as a positive role model, these teens are more likely to turn to crime. And so the vicious cycle of the next generation turning to crime continues, further upping the economic costs to society.

Not only is the problem of single moms raising their kids a growing one, but so is the number of women who are pregnant and give birth while they are incarcerated. One-third of women entering jail or prison are pregnant and have to give their children up right after birth, resulting in further societal damage.[212] These children end up in foster care if no grandparent or other relative steps forward. The loss of a child is so devastating that it can contribute to recidivism among women prisoners, whereas if they were allowed to keep their children, those children could give them a reason to turn their lives around.

Moreover, when children are raised without their parents, this can contribute to the children turning to crime as they grow up, especially if they are shuttled around in the foster care system from family to family. They may be especially likely to join gangs because they are drawn to the strong bonds that create a family-like sense of belonging. And as gang members, they may be drawn into a series of crimes and gang battles that plague the inner cities that are characterized by these damaged family units. This perpetuation of the urban ghetto represents one more social and economic cost of current incarceration policies.

Accordingly, these costs to families, the local social structure, and society as a whole have to be taken into

---

[212] Pfaff, *Locked In*, 2017, p. 172.

account in devising criminal justice system reforms.[213] These reforms are necessary not just as a response to liberal concerns to create a system that is more sympathetic to the problems faced by black women and their children. Indeed, in addition to the costs of black male incarceration, welfare moms and impoverished children represent an economic drain on taxpayers, not to mention an erosion of family values. Worst of all, the family disruption that results from incarceration threatens to breed criminals from the next generation. So the current approach has hidden societal and economic costs far beyond those of police, prosecution, courts, and incarceration. Reforms are critical to stop the breeding of more criminals in our urban ghettos and to reduce costs that might otherwise go for dealing with higher priority violent crime or other worthwhile societal endeavors.

It is very likely that crime and our corrections system have become intertwined in a vicious cycle. The concentration of crime in poor urban black communities has led to both disproportionate rates of incarceration of young black males and to a fragmentation of black society in those ghettos. Kerik, no bleeding heart liberal, states that "the U.S. criminal justice system will be substantially responsible for the destruction of inner-city kids, black males primarily, if things don't change."[214]

Single moms do the best they can to raise their children, but without adequate adult male role models, their sons are likely to drop out of school, become prey for gangs, or engage in illegal activities that get them arrested and imprisoned. Their single mom task is made all the more

---

[213] Pfaff, *Locked In*, 2017, p.119
[214] Kerik, *From Jailer to Jailed*, p. 260.

difficult since nearly a quarter of them are jobless. As a result, many live below the poverty line, half living in extreme poverty, a third being food insecure, and nearly half receiving food stamps.[215] The situation is epidemic in the black community. In 2013, 72% of all births to black women were to unmarried women.[216]

At the same time, their daughters, used to seeing their moms somehow manage without husbands, are more prone to becoming young single moms themselves.

[215] Dawn Lee, "Single Mother Statistics", Single Mother Guide, 9/27/2017; https://singlemotherguide/single-mother-statistics
[216] "Births to Unmarried Women", Child Trends/Databank Indicator; www.childtrends.org/indicators/births-to-unmarried-women

If the young black males leaving prison haven't been adequately rehabilitated and don't find jobs, the cycle persists. They commit crimes to survive, get arrested, and end up in jail or prison once more.

According to usually conservative[217] *New York Times* columnist David Brooks, the problem in the black community is not due to deadbeat dads but rather to a failure to take adequate contraceptive measures in less-than-loving relationships that are not destined to succeed. These relationships fall apart within a year or two after childbirth. Brooks' remedy: "find someone you love before you have intercourse."[218] Presumably the result would be more children born within established marriages, which would help kids grow up in stable families. Thus, they wouldn't be left to grow up on the streets to turn to crime, which would reduce crime and save the country money in the process. However, this may be naïve since black values may not be the same as whites', and there has been a serious rise in white teenage pregnancies despite "Just Say No" pledges.

Some Reasons for High Recidivism

One big problem that prisoners face when they are released is the lack of preparedness and support they receive upon getting out to a world without the extensive structure they have grown accustomed to in prison. This lack of preparedness and support contributes to the high recidivism rate. While ex-cons are also subject to many confining rules

---

[217] but he did support Obama
[218] David Brooks, "Why fathers leave", *Arkansas Democrat-Gazette,* 6/19/2017.

and regulations ordinary citizens would find abhorrent, those rules and regulations may actually provide them some structure. If they have help in changing their behaviors and better adjusting to the world outside on release, they will be more successful in avoiding a return to prison. Therefore, it makes good economic sense to put more money into providing this support and structure for ex-cons leaving prison.

One guide to achieving success after prison is *Beyond Bars, Rejoining Society after Prison* by Jeffrey Ian Ross and Stephen C. Richards,[219] which was written to guide convicts about to reenter society. Read from the perspective of an outsider, this insightful book reveals why recidivism is so high, given what released prisoners have to face both in prison and when they get out. One obstacle is that prisoners who are adjusted to prison life, where they have little or no freedom and no responsibility, have to swiftly readjust to a system where they have both.

Fortunately, most prisoners aren't forced to adjust to the real world "cold turkey," where they are put back on the street with few resources, other than about $200 in walking around money[220] – too little to get back on their feet economically without outside help. Though they do get some help from probation and parole case workers, it is not enough by itself. Commonly, many are put on parole long-term and required to stay for several months in halfway houses. There they learn some reentry skills and get some assistance in obtaining initial employment. But the jobs they get are

---

[219] Jeffrey Ian Ross and Stephen C. Richards, *Beyond Bars, Rejoining Society after Prison,* Alpha, 2009.
[220] In fact, many states provide far less, and some none at all: James Kilgore, *Understanding Mass Incarceration: A People's Guide to the Key Civil Rights Struggle of Our Time,* The New Press, 2015, p. 98.

minimum wage, and their wages are paid to the halfway houses and frequently garnished. The halfway houses also vary in quality, and some are in poor inner-city environments, where the prisoners are exposed to the criminal underworld involved with drugs and other crimes on surrounding streets. Nicer neighborhoods don't want halfway houses in their back yards.[221]

Another big problem leading to recidivism is that the parole system is often oppressive, and many ex-prisoners have their rights taken away permanently. Their parole officer can make unannounced visits. If guns, alcohol or drugs are found in the household they are staying in, even if these items are not theirs, they generally get hauled off back to prison for technical violation of their parole. This happens to about one-third of all parolees.[199,222] Meanwhile, many, if not most inmates have been forgotten and forsaken by their families, and all their possessions have disappeared.

Other barriers, such as a denial of civil rights, a lack of eligibility to receive federal housing, and a requirement to reveal their ex-prison status, also make it difficult for ex-convicts to adjust to the real world. There are many such barriers to their successful re-entry back into society, increasing the odds they will fail, even though a large percentage of Americans favor a removal of these barriers.

For example, 74% of all Americans, including 62% of conservatives and Republicans and 64% of Tea Party voters, feel that once these prisoners have served their time, they should be allowed to vote.[223] For the most part, they also feel

---

[221] Jeffrey Ian Ross and Stephen C. Richards, *Beyond Bars, Rejoining Society after Prison,* Alpha, 2009.
[222] Pfaff, *Locked In,* 2017, pp 39-40.
[223] "Agreed: Serve Your Time, Cast Your Ballot," *New York Times*, October 30, 2016.

that ex-cons should have other rights restored on the grounds they have paid their debt to society and should be given another chance to follow the straight and narrow.

However, currently they still face these barriers:

❖ felons cannot vote,
❖ felons cannot receive federal housing, and
❖ felons most often must divulge that they have been to prison to potential employers, and this admission greatly decreases their job prospects,[224] since many prospective employers fear becoming a victim of ex-cons.

This requirement to reveal their ex-con status has been subjected to considerable scrutiny recently, with a view to eliminating this requirement, since it has limited the ability of ex-cons to find jobs and get reintegrated into society.[225] To this end, some localities have "banned the box" on job applications. But for the most part, ex-cons still have to admit their former imprisonment. If they don't, once this omission has been discovered, which is likely given that more than 80% of employers perform criminal background checks,[226] this is grounds for instant dismissal. Unfortunately, one unintended consequence of banning the box is that employers have become less likely to interview *any* black applicants, since they are apt to assume that blacks are more likely to be ex-cons.[227]

---

[224] National Institute of Justice, "Research on Reentry and Employment", https://www.nij.gov/topics/corrections/reentry/pages/employment.aspx
[225] Jordan Segall, "Mass Incarceration, Ex-felon Discrimination & Black Labor Market Disadvantage," *University of Pennsylvania Journal of Law and Social Change*, vol. 14,159-182, 2011
[226] National Institute of Justice, "Research on Reentry and Employment," https://www.nij.gov/topics/corrections/reentry/pages/employment.aspx
[227] "An Effort to Stop Discrimination May Actually Increase It," *New York Times*, August 21, 2016.

This negative attitudes of employers towards ex-cons, and especially blacks whom they suspect of being ex-cons, is an especially difficult barrier to overcome for the nearly half of ex-cons who are black. This unfortunate situation occurs because only about 40% of employers are likely to hire ex-offenders,[228] and employer callbacks for black ex-offenders applying for a job are only 15% compared to 28% for white ex-offenders.[229] The result is a much reduced income for a high percentage of ex-cons and their families, if they have managed to reconnect with them.

To illustrate, in one study of ex-cons in Chicago, Cleveland, and Houston, ex-offenders were more than twice as likely as individuals without a record to be dependent on income from family and friends than on legal employment two months after release. Eight months later, they were still more dependent on their family, since their median monthly income was only $700. They were only more likely to be employed under certain conditions: if they were married, held a job in the six months before prison, held a prison job or participated in a job training program in prison, or used a former employer to find a job.[230] Most of these same conditions also contributed to their being less likely to return to prison, since reincarceration was less likely if they had worked in the six months before prison, earned money two months after release, participated in job training in prison, or held a job while in prison.[231]

---

[228] John Schmitt and Kris Warner, "Ex-offenders and the Labor Market", Center for Economic Policy and Research, November, 2010.
[229] https://www.nij.gov/topics/corrections/reentry/pages/employment.aspx
[230] "Employment after Prison: A Longitudinal Study of Releases in Three States", Urban Institute, Justice Policy Center, Research Brief, 10/2008.
[231] Ibid.

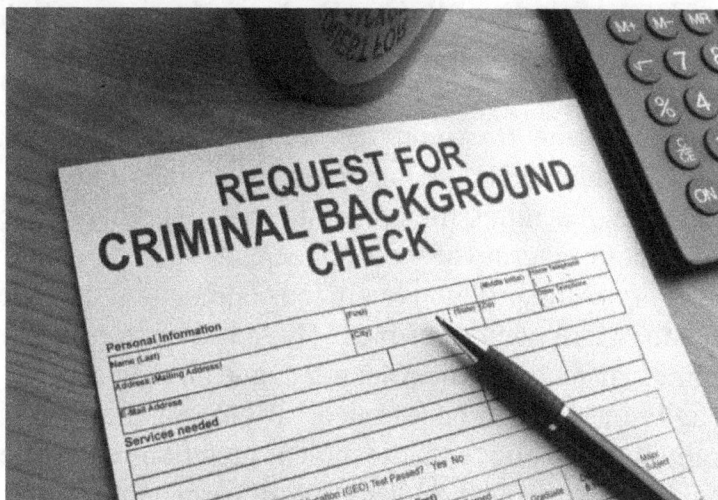

Thus, employment substantially reduces the risk of recidivism. Yet more than 60% of ex-cons remain jobless their first year after release,[232] their most vulnerable time for committing a crime or a violation of their release which will send them back to prison.

The publicly accessible offender database also contributes to recidivism, since it makes it more difficult to successfully reenter society. That's because a publicly accessible offender registry makes it easy for anyone checking to discover if a person seeking a job has a record. And anyone who is using a cell-phone or has a Facebook or Twitter account can easily spread information on the ex-con's record far and wide. This makes it much more difficult for ex-cons to be accepted back into society. It is as if they are wearing the modern-day version of the "Scarlet Letter" on their chest -- or in this case, in a modern database -- for all to see and shame them for their time in prison.

---

[232] National Institute of Justice, "Research on Reentry and Employment", https://www.nij.gov/topics/corrections/reentry/pages/employment.aspx

Reducing Recidivism Reduces Incarceration

A good way to reduce recidivism is to simply reduce the incarceration of ex-convicts for minor technical violations of parole which could be handled by warnings and fines. The alternative of sending them back to prison has been much costlier both in terms of their upkeep, as well as preventing them from being productive citizens and making it more likely they will commit crimes. There is a consensus among criminologists that some prisoners have already served enough time and can be released. Therefore, these criminologists believe that technical violations of parole should not by themselves lead to re-incarceration in prisons.

As extensive research shows, if less severe sanctions were imposed for technical violations of parole, this could reduce recidivism by one-third,[233] and that change in policy would have a major effect to reduce the number of incarcerated.

Reductions in recidivism alone can make a substantial dent on our prison population. The following chart indicates how significantly reducing recidivism can decrease the prison population.[234]

---

[233] John Pfaff, *Locked In*, 2017, pp 39-40

[234] We start with 1.53 million in prison and that technical violations of parole will reduce to some extent the proportion of those released from prison who return to prison. Recent data indicate 41.9% of all prisoners (641,000) are released annually, 55% of whom are expected to be reincarcerated within 5 years; together with 631,000 new admissions to prison (352,000 recidivists and 279,000 first time offenders).

Effect of Reducing Recidivism
on Prison Population

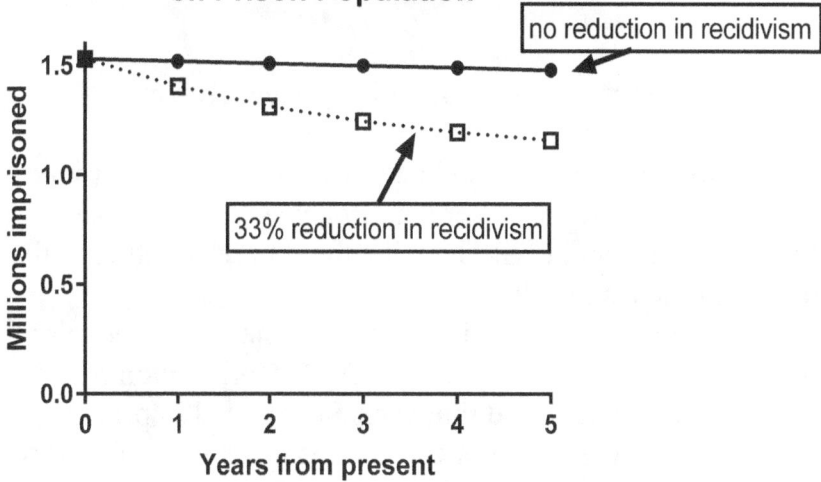

As the chart shows, there is a declining prison population for each year that a strategy of reducing recidivism by 33% is put in place. This could be accomplished solely by eliminating imprisonments for technical violations of parole. [235] From a zero reduction when the strategy is first initiated, after five years, the millions of individuals imprisoned goes down by nearly 25%, from 1.53 million to 1.16 million.

Translated into money saved, that reduction in incarceration could represent $15-20 billion a year[236] out of the costs of upkeep for those individuals unnecessarily imprisoned, plus untold billions more for the loss of their

---

[235] The upper solid line labeled continues the trend of 10,000 more inmates released than entering prison. The dotted line shows the effects of a 33% reduction in returns to prison.

[236] a quarter of our current costs, if we managed to close a quarter of our prisons

productivity and the cost to the family and community for more crimes committed by them.

Some Ways to Reduce Recidivism

So now the question becomes -- what to do to reduce recidivism. There are several approaches that have been found to work, and I will describe them here, together with new approaches that should work.

Providing training in prison was the key to reducing recidivism, according to a 2013 RAND Corporation report.[237] Their findings suggested that each $1 invested in prison education saved $4-$5 in incarceration costs in the first three years following release. This investment involved spending only about $1600 per inmate, a minor additional cost relative to the $20,000-$30,000 yearly cost of imprisoning one inmate.

The results were spectacular. Inmates participating in education programs reduced their odds of returning to prison by 43%. Their post-release percentage of employment was 13% higher if they participated in education or vocational programs, and 28% higher if they had vocational training.[238]

Perhaps another alternative to reducing recidivism, given all the obstacles listed previously, is for ex-cons to enlist in the military, since doing so is not always prevented by a single misdemeanor or felony. One advantage of enlisting is that the military can offer a strictly regimented

---

[237] Lois M. Davis, Robert Bozick, Jennifer Steele, Jessica Saunders and Jeremy Miles,"Education and Vocational Training in Prisons Reduces Recidivism, Improves Job Outlook", RAND, News Release 8/22/2013, http://www.rand.org/news/press/2013/08/22.html
[238] Ibid.

environment that ex-cons might readily adapt to, since they have already faced a highly structured environment in prison. The emphasis on teamwork in the military might substitute for the tendency to join gangs. Most prisoners join gangs in order to feel a greater sense of belonging or to feel more safety and security by being in a group of fellow-prisoners who are protecting each other. Basic training in the military thus reduces the motivation to join gangs and teaches ex-cons to look out for their fellow soldiers regardless of their ethnicity or background.

A related suggestion is to create a class of "boot camp" programs in which younger inmates can volunteer for a tough, strenuous program which teaches them military discipline and teamwork. Why volunteer? One good incentive is to reduce their sentence for good behavior. That's what a program at Rikers Island jail that Bernard Kerik established did. It offered the carrot of reducing a sentence from 12 months down to 6 months, if the prisoners completed the program.[239]

Below are some of the possible additional approaches to reducing recidivism, since there is no single fix. But adopting many of these fixes is needed to keep down the prison population and reduce costs. Such fixes will also provide new hope and job opportunities to the many men who are released from prison to keep them from returning to a life of crime, only to be arrested and returned to prison again. Given the alternative -- more crime, more incarceration, more recidivism -- both state and federal governments have begun investing in rehabilitation programs to reduce the recidivism rate. Some examples of these programs are described below.

---

[239] Kerik, *From Jailer to Jailed,* p. 261.

Education Programs for Prisoners

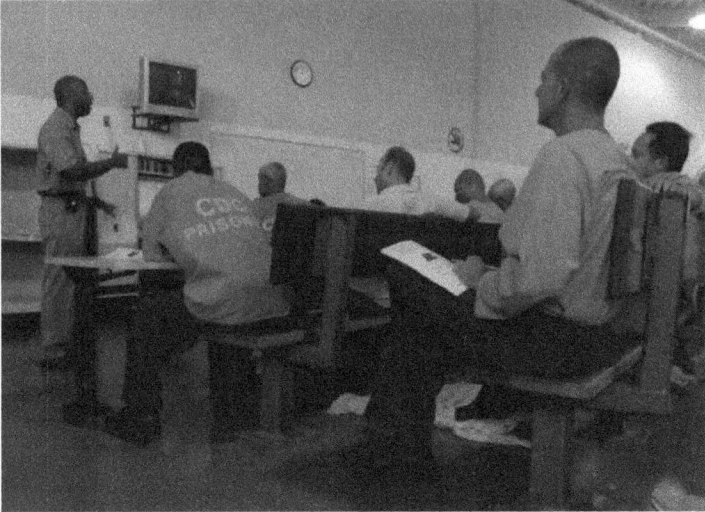

A number of programs have been designed to help prisoners get the education they need to obtain work and avoid returning to crime to survive. Such programs can help prisoners overcome the many barriers they face to getting an education, most notably a lack of income and family support.

Some of these educational programs seem promising and should be encouraged, since a 2013 RAND Corporation study concluded that a prisoner's involvement in a prisoner education program reduced that person's odds of returning to prison by 43% and saved over $4 for each $1 spent.[240]

It is especially important to encourage or even require inmates to participate in programs to earn a high school degree or GED equivalent, since most prisoners haven't graduated from high school, and doing so will greatly

---

[240] "Education and Vocational Training in Prisons Reduces Recidivism, Improves Job Outlook", RAND Corporation, 8/22/2013, http://www.rand.org/news/press/2013/08/22.html

enhance their job prospects when released. It is not necessary to provide college classes, since most inmates would not be eligible to enroll in college programs, and taxpayers are likely to resist federal support for them. Thus college programs are unlikely to affect many of the 1.5 million U.S. prisoners,

Current Programs Aimed at Reducing Recidivism

A number of programs around the country which emphasize rehabilitation have also helped to reduce recidivism. These programs are initiated in the final year or so of imprisonment, using an approach which has resulted in positive outcomes in European prisons, as described in Chapter 3.

These programs reflect a number of different approaches adapted to different groups of prisoners -- and regardless of the exact method, these seem to work. For example, some programs are faith-based, some are apolitical, and others involve alliances between corporate donors and liberal social workers. For instance, Koch Industries, a conservative industry group much maligned by liberals, came together with the ACLU[241] to promote overhauling the criminal justice system, under the group's name: the Coalition for Public Safety.[242] The program, which has been operating

---

[241] American Civil Liberties Union

[242] It is refreshing that groups like Koch Industries on the right and ACLU on the left can work together more constructively than our elected politicians. Perhaps compromise is not extinct after all, merely on the list of endangered species. Political and public discourse in the U.S. has been squeezed into sound bites, tweets and slogans which divide us too much, sometimes in seemingly contradictory ways. Take the example of Pro-Life and Pro-Choice. I have little doubt that many Pro-Life, anti-abortion advocates are in favor of the death penalty, while Pro-Choice

since 2015, supports programs to promote reentry, as well as other reforms.[243] It provides a successful bipartisan model for other groups on different sides of the political spectrum to follow to reduce recidivism and the costs in and out of prison that go with it.

Community reintegration programs are another successful approach, which I have discussed in some of my previous books, including *American Justice?* and *The Price of Justice in America.* In *American Justice?,* I mentioned Project Return, a successful community-based program in Nashville, Tennessee, which provides numerous pre- and post-release services for convicts, including housing referrals, medical referrals, food assistance, transportation passes, and more.

In *The Price of Justice in America*, I mentioned successful reintegration programs developed at San Quentin in California that have gotten a buy-in for participation by 75% of the inmates there. Among other things, the programs offer them therapy for anger management and drug addiction, as well as training in print and radio communications and in software programming.

Another promising program in is Women in Recovery, an Oklahoma program which helps women with drug addiction and mental health problems re-bond with their children and families. This intensive outpatient program lasts nearly 18 months and costs about $20,000 per inmate, less than the cost of continued incarceration, with recidivism declining sharply to less than 5%.[244]

Another program with favorable results is New York City's Prison-to-College Pipeline for helping both

---

abortion advocates willing to terminate fetuses are unwilling to support the death penalty for murderers.
[243] PBS News Hour 4/30/15
[244] "Mothers in Prison," *New York Times,* 11/27/2016.

incarcerated and formerly incarcerated prisoners, even if the students have to take on student loans. The state has committed $7.5 million to offer classes to 1000 inmates over the next 5 years.[245]

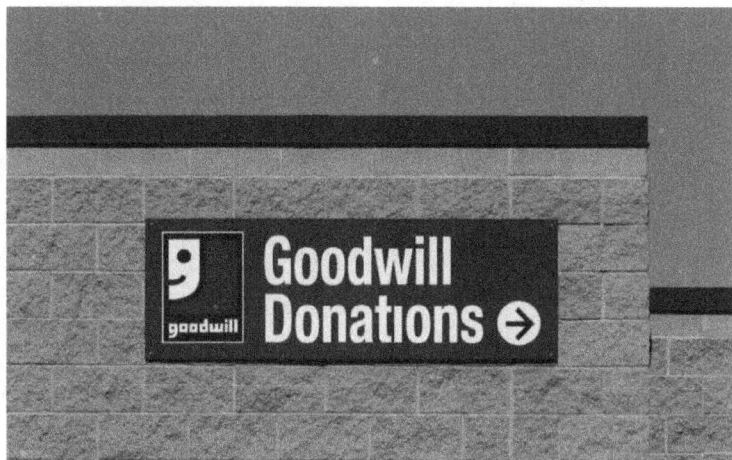

One of the most promising rehabilitation programs for released prisoners is that offered by Goodwill Industries, which I only became aware of as this book was being edited. They have been advocates for ex-offender rehabilitation for many years and even published a 67-page document in 2008 entitled "The Road to Reintegration. Goodwill Industries' Call to Action to Ensure Successful Re-Entry for Ex-Offenders".[246] This remarkable document makes many of the

---

[245] "Prison-to-College Pipeline", Prisoner Reentry Institute, John Jay College of Criminal Justice; http://johnjaypri.org/educational-initiatives/prison-to-college-pipeline/
[246] Charisse Lyons, "The Road to Reintegration. Goodwill Industries' Call to Action to Ensure Successful Re-entry for Ex-Offenders", Goodwill Industries International, Inc., 11/2008; https://www.goodwill.org/wp-content/uploads/2014/12/Road-to-Reintegration-Full.pdf ; I am very grateful to Pastor Katherine Williams of Little Rock for making me aware of their program.

same points made in this book. It also covers others such as child support, mothers losing their children to foster care, how ex-prisoners with mental health issues do far worse after release, and how much costlier it is to incarcerate elderly prisoners with health issues than younger prisoners, topics not covered here.

Starting from Goodwill Industries' philosophy of "a hand up, not a hand out," the report details how in 2005 Goodwill had 97 agencies serving 45,000 ex-offenders, which increased to 119 agencies serving 82,132 in 2007. No doubt the numbers are much higher now. Its Executive Summary makes three main points:

> "Goodwill Industries believes that providing job placement and employment services to ex-offenders is a cornerstone toward building a prisoner re-entry continuum that holds offenders accountable for their actions, yet supports them when they return to their communities."

> "Goodwill Industries believes that access to safe and stable housing is another cornerstone in the prisoner re-entry continuum."

> "Goodwill Industries believes that until necessary steps are taken to help former prisoners attain and retain jobs, recidivism will continue to be an escalating problem that weakens families and communities and stretches states' correction budgets to the breaking point."

For most citizens, this means that you don't even need to donate money to help this cause. Your donations of unneeded or unwanted household items will help this cause, as well as all the other causes Goodwill champions.

What offers great potential is that Goodwill exists all over the country. In principle therefore, the success of initiatives at one location could much more readily be implemented at another. Unfortunately, it is not clear whether that is being done, and a great opportunity might be being missed.

Another nationwide program that helps ex-offenders to find jobs is the Salvation Army. The different Salvation Army offices may interact and communicate better than Goodwill centers, but most folk are more inclined to give financial donations to the Salvation Army, particularly when their holiday kettles are out at many locations. The Salvation Army does have household donation centers, but not as many as Goodwill.

In addition, local programs around the country offer jobs to recently released former convicts. For instance, MaineWorks offers former convicts, whose crimes involved substance abuse disorders, not only temporary jobs, but it helps the ex-cons secure housing and even transportation. Ex-prisoners can remain in the program even if they relapse, as long as they get medical help or sign up for a bed in a sober house. The goal is to prepare them for placement in more permanent jobs. So far the program has helped over 70 ex-prisoners in Maine, and it has been expanding into other states.[247]

Here around Little Rock, one program which claims success is Pathway to Freedom, a faith-based 18-month, in-prison program, after which prisoners experience another year of mentoring and re-entry assistance after their release.[248] The

---

[247] "Giving Ex-inmates a Job, and a Ride to Work," *New York Times* 9/4/2016.
[248] Eric Besson, "Arkansas Program Aims to Prevent Repeat Prison Stays", *U.S. News & World Report*, 3/28/2017;

program was developed from the Prison Fellowship initiative founded by former Richard Nixon aide Charles Colson, after he became an evangelist while in prison.[249]

This program receives both private and state funding and spends only about $450,000 annually, but the Arkansas Department of Corrections supplies the food, housing and health care. The program already has a number of successful graduates. It reports 893 enrollees, 291 who have completed all 18 months. It also reports 115 successful program graduates for the full 30 month program, of which only 15% have been jailed again so far.[250]

While the program is extremely successful in helping those who complete the program, so far only a minority of ex-

https://www.usnews.com/news/best-states/arkansas/articles/2017-03-26/arkansas-program-aims-to-prevent-repeat-prison-stays
[249] Dagan and Telles, *Prison Break*, Oxford University Press, 2016.
[250] Eric Besson, "Program Sets Inmates on a New Path", *Pressreader*, 3/19/2017; https://www.pressreader.com/usa/arkansas-democrat-gazette/20170319/281479276231678

convicts participate, and it is uncertain how many of the participants would have avoided recidivism on their own. Nevertheless, in view of the apparent success of this program for Christian prisoners, it would be worth considering similar faith-based programs for Muslims, since more than a third of black convicts are Muslim or convert to Islam in prison.[251] However, such programs should be closely monitored to ensure no Islamic radicalism ideology is spread.

Another program in Little Rock for ex-offenders preparing for release is Compassion in Action, which lasts for twelve weeks.[252] It provides job training, education, and mentoring, and it claims to reduce recidivism by 90%.

Arkansas also has a Drug and Alcohol Recovery Program, which affords opportunities for employment for ex-convicts, but it has recently been criticized for sending all wages to programs for rent, food and rehabilitation services, which lawyers contended amounted to "slavery." As an unfortunate result, one Republican State Senator has withdrawn his company from the program.[253]

Additionally, the Little Rock government has established a re-entry program, whereby it hires local rehabilitated ex-prisoner graduates into a number of positions in city departments. These placements have included hiring ex-convicts into the Fire and Police departments, in several

---

[251] "One in Three Black Inmates Converts to Islam in Prison." *DailyCaller.com;* http://conservative-headlines.com/2014/11/one-in-three-blacks-inmates-converts-to-islam-in-prison

[252] Cary Jenkins, "Sherman Tate Takes Ribbing to Benefit Re-Entry Program," *Arkansas Democrat-Gazette*, 7/2/2017.

[253] Nathan Owens, "Senator's Firm Sheds Rehab Program," *Arkansas Democrat-Gazette*, 11/1/17.

city government departments, at the zoo, and for mowing and landscape maintenance.[254]

Some Arkansas industrial firms with high turnover have programs to hire ex-convicts, too, and the firms have generally found them to be good workers. A rubber plant in Springdale hired 10 work-release inmates and parolees. They were reliable, cut employee turnover down from 50% annually to only 15%, and allowed the inmates to save up money that will be very useful upon their release.[255]

Still another Little Rock program is a Second Chance Pell Grant program that allows prisoners to obtain high school diplomas or their equivalent in GED degrees. Today, over 50 students attend a Second Chance Pell Grant program run by Arkansas State University at Newport, which has proved very successful.[256]

The Storybook Project of Arkansas offers a program which records convicts reading storybooks for their children, which helps the convicts maintain connections with their own children.[257]

---

[254] Chelsea Boozer, "Ex-Criminal Offenders Hired for Little Rock's Re-Entry Crews. Work in Departments Gives Residents a Second Chance." *Arkansas Democrat-Gazette*, 10/17/2016.

[255] Doug Thompson, "Convicts filling employee need in tight market. Work-release inmates prove to be reliable, company says", *Arkansas Democrat-Gazette*, 12/29/2016.

[256] "ASUN Participates in Second Chance Pell Program", Arkansas State University-Newport, 7/5/2016; http://www.asun.edu/news/1269/asun-participates-second-chance-pell-program

[257] Kerik is certainly in favor of any programs that increase connections of inmates with their children: Kerik, *From Jailer to Jailed*, p.283-4.

In sum, there are many of these small programs in many communities, including in Arkansas, where I have shown a wide variety of examples. Though these are individually small programs, they add up, resulting in potentially thousands of ex-convicts that benefit from such programs each year.[258] And the more lives that are touched by such programs, the less likely these ex-convicts are to commit new crimes and return to prison. The cost savings from reduced recidivism can be substantial, as mentioned earlier.

Legislation Dealing with Recidivism

Aside from ongoing programs, a number of states have passed legislation aimed at reducing recidivism. For example, in Arkansas, in April 2017, the state legislature

---

[258] A longer list of such programs in each of the 50 states can be accessed at http://www.helpforfelons.org/reentry-programs-ex-offenders-state

passed Act 423, the Criminal Justice Efficiency and Safety Act. This act has a lot to like, as summarized in a local paper -- a boon for citizens, since the legal language in the bill makes it hard for the average citizen to understand.[259]

One big positive is that the act replaces sending ex-cons with technical violations of parole and probation to prison with sending them to Arkansas Community Correction facilities for 45 to 90 days for rehabilitative programming. The result of this change in the law is that sending ex-cons to rehab instead of prison may free up as many as 1600 prison beds, saving Arkansas $30-40 million. The legislation also establishes several regional Crisis Stabilization Units, where people who have committed nuisance offenses can go for several days of treatment, if they were high on drugs or having a mental health crisis. Such units will also reduce jail and prison populations.

Additionally, the act requires crisis intervention training for law enforcement officers in order to de-escalate potential confrontational interactions with individuals with mental health problems. While additional new parole and probation officers were recommended to reduce the current average caseload of 125 cases, the parole and probation departments may not receive sufficient funding to implement hiring these officers. At least the legislation shows the lawmakers' intent in seeking to reduce unnecessary imprisonment by directing certain low-level offending ex-convicts to rehabilitation rather than back to prison.

Still other bills in Arkansas provide other pathways to rehabilitation and reduced recidivism. One such bill allows

---

[259] Benjamin Hardy, David Koon, Lindsey Millar and Leslie Newell Peacock, "Mean. Nasty. Brutish. And short-sighted, for the most part. But it could have been worse at the Capitol": Lindsey Millar, "Criminal Justice. Actual reform", *Arkansas Times* 4/13/2017,

those convicted of a felony drug offense to receive Temporary Assistance for Needy Families benefits. The bill also permits those with suspended drivers' licenses due to unpaid fines or fees to continue to drive to school or work, as long as the original offense did not involve a motor vehicle. Additionally, the law prevents minors from being sentenced to life without the possibility of parole.

Conservative legislators are giving this legislation favoring rehabilitation a strong endorsement, given its ability to reduce costs and crime. For example, the Republican State Senator chair of the state Senate Judiciary Committee, Jeremy Hutchinson, stated: "Longer sentences do not, in fact, result in lower crime rates. The longer [people are] incarcerated, the greater chance of recidivism they have." Given this view, Hutchinson fought to defeat a three strikes bill which would have required anyone with three stints in prison to serve at least 80% of any subsequent sentence. The bill would have increased the prison population and cost several hundred million dollars.

Changes in Policy to Provide More Rehabilitation

These new legislative regulations have led to changes in policy in the local departments of corrections to provide more rehabilitation services. For example, following the lead of the legislature, the Arkansas Board of Corrections will be sending some technical violators of parole and probation who fail drug tests or commit certain misdemeanor offenses to

Community Corrections facilities for 45-180 days of supervision instead of prison.[260]

More funds have also been provided to community groups contributing to the rehabilitation effort. One example is Restore Hope, a nonprofit group helping communities meet the needs of prison inmates returning home and foster children needing homes. In June 2017, it was one of the two recipients to receive the most money from Republican Arkansas Governor Asa Hutchinson's Emergency Fund to support its mission.[261]

Some Problems in Reducing Recidivism Rates

Yet, despite the many gains in promoting rehabilitation to reduce recidivism, there are still a number of challenges and barriers to be overcome. One big problem is that many ex-convicts do commit new crimes, and there is little difference in Arkansas, as in many other states, between these recidivism rates for blacks and whites or between offenders who committed violent or non-violent offenses. They might all be considered equal opportunity offenders.

In Arkansas as in other states, many more recidivists return to prison as a result of a new sentence (63%) compared to those who return as a result of a technical violation of parole (37%). While the proportion of ex-convicts returning to the Arkansas Department of Corrections (DOC) declines slowly with age, from a peak of returning ex-cons aged 18 to 24, there is no major drop down to less than half this peak

---

[260] John Moritz, "Prison Board Oks plan for parole, probation violators", *Arkansas Democrat-Gazette*, 6/27/2017.
[261] Michael R. Wickline, "Governor allots funds for 3 private colleges. Money to provide students grant aid", *Arkansas Democrat-Gazette*, 6/18/2017

number until after age 55. In other words, the vast majority of returning convicts committing new offenses are young adults, and a key reason for their return to crime is that many of them move back to their old stomping grounds. There they can readily connect up with their old buddies with whom they engaged in crime before, and since they have difficulty finding jobs or otherwise reintegrating into the community, they have an incentive to commit crimes again. The Arkansas Department of Corrections explains this conundrum well when it notes that, "Inmates, especially parolees, are likely to return to the same impoverished neighborhoods that substantially increase criminal opportunities; limit educational, vocational, and social support services; and attenuate personal support networks."[262]

This lack of reintegration back into the community is a major problem in reducing recidivism rates, and ex-cons needed extra help to overcome the resistance they face, most notably in getting jobs and being accepted in local community groups. Senator Joyce Elliot, a black Democrat, pointed up this problem in a blog in the *Arkansas Times,* where she stated that "the state's corrections system is good, but its reintegration system is nonexistent." While the *Times* is a liberal paper, her argument is equally relevant for conservatives, and there is growing support within the criminal justice community for such policy changes.

For example, Kevin Murphy, the Director of the Arkansas Department of Community Correction, recommended establishing re-entry centers across the state for housing inmates 6-9 months away from the end of their sentence. Such centers could help to prepare them for reentry by providing them with intense employment and family

---

[262] Tiffany Compton, Jacob M. Laan, and Brittani McNeal, "Arkansas Department of Correction Recidivism Study," September, 2015.

counseling. As a further perk, Murphy recommended combining this housing help with a tax credit program to encourage employers to hire offenders who have gone through such a program.[263]

What Else Can Be Done to Reduce Recidivism?

Regrettably, each of the programs described here assist only a handful of ex-convicts at a time -- not enough to put a significant dent in recidivism unless many more such programs are implemented around the country. So what else should be done?

In *Beyond Bars*, Ross and Richards suggest that performance measures of prison programs to reduce recidivism should be evaluated to determine what programs are working and what ones are less effective. These evaluation outcomes would encourage more emphasis on prison programs aimed at reducing recidivism, rather than just housing prisoners through their sentences.[264]

Ross and Richards also suggest that the basic financial needs of released prisoners should be met for three months to give them a chance to start life afresh. Former prisoners also need help in finding better jobs or in getting some financial support while they get back on their feet, since currently minimum wage jobs earning less than $16,000 annually are

---

[263] Benjamin Hardy, Arkansas Blog, "Recidivism Rate Among Arkansas Parolees Is 57 Percent, Says Corrections Official," *Arkansas Times*,12/2/14; http://www.arktimes.com/ArkansasBlog/archives/2014/12/02/recidivism-rate-among-arkansas-parolees-is-57-percent-says-corrections-official
[264] Jeffrey Ian Ross and Stephen C. Richards, *Beyond Bars, Rejoining Society after Prison*, Alpha, 2009.

all that are usually available to newly released ex-convicts. Compared to the cost of continued housing in prison ($20,000-$30,000 annually), a three-month investment of $4000 per prisoner in some pilot program would seem a worthwhile investment to determine if it would reduce recidivism. The $4000 could even be considered a loan, to be repaid on a certain schedule, or it could be added to the prisoner's debt if he is re-incarcerated.

Because many prisoners had or still have substance abuse problems upon release, Ross and Richards recommend that one prison per state be turned into a Residential Treatment Center. This Center could have a professionally trained staff, be open to the public as well as to ex-convicts for treatment of 3-6 months, and be paid for by the state or perhaps funded through private charitable contributions. If open to the public, this Center could also help treat the rampant methamphetamine and exploding opiate epidemics ravaging the country, which would diminish the legitimate resentment that taxpayers feel about convicts getting special treatment. Many citizens feel such resentment because we don't now have enough treatment centers accessible to low income individuals in need. However, once it is shown that such Centers contribute to reducing recidivism and incarceration costs, this will likely reduce community resistance to including ex-convicts in such programs.

One way to fund such Centers might be through social impact bonds involving the private sector, which would reduce or eliminate the costs to taxpayers of such programs. In addition to being promoted as a contribution to the community, these programs could be set up like an investment, whereby the success of the programs would enable funders to receive a payout tied to the financial savings or gains provided by the program.[265] For example, if a treatment center is able to reduce recidivism and incarceration expenses by X amount, the funders would receive a percentage of those saved or earned funds. This would represent a way to profit by doing good.

Another suggestion is to teach prisoners how to start small farms and provide them with some of the basic tools to operate these farms. Such an approach has already been implemented successfully for veterans. Under this program, farming skills could be taught in a rural prison environment, and the prisoners could also be taught the kind of attitude or mindset required to be successful. For example, farming requires perseverance and stamina. Prisoners could be taught this much needed attitude and endurance, which many don't have -- one of their failings, leading them to seek the get rich quick approach to crime that has led them to prison. Additionally, farming encourages teamwork, since prisoners will have to work together to plant and care for the crops. Such farming programs have been successful in training military veterans[266] and they could readily be adapted for ex-felons or include them along with veterans.

Another advantage of teaching prisoners to farm is they generally will have to leave behind the city environment that has proved to be a breeding ground for their criminal activity. They will generally have to leave, since farming normally requires a rural environment, except for some farming specialties, such as hydroponics or some small urban community gardens. Thus, learning to farm in the country may be just what ex-convicts need to turn their lives around

---

[265] Pfaff, *Locked In,* 2017, p. 230.
[266] Nathan Owens, "Military veterans find farming's a good fit. Program's stints offer them a taste of rural life", *Arkansas Democrat-Gazette,* 6/18/2017.

and keep them away from their former urban ghetto environment and reuniting with their criminal buddies.

The prisoners in these programs who undergo the required training could then be given the extra help they need to get started in whatever business or work they train for. For instance, they could apply for bank loans to get started, and these could be guaranteed by local or state government. Providing such loans might be an ideal approach for helping prisoners get involved in a farming business after they get out of prison, especially since many prisoners already work on prison farms.

Similar support could help ex-prisoners succeed in other businesses, after they successfully go through a training program in prison.[267] For instance, a prisoner who learns how to bake in prison could be given a loan to start a small bakery after leaving prison. A prisoner who learns about becoming an auto mechanic, plumber, painter, or other trade might be given access to a small loan to open up a shop in the community. In this way, the prisoner could build on the skills learned in prison to transition into productive and profitable work.

Finally, Kerik recommends that those who have paid their debt to society have their civil and constitutional rights returned and their convictions removed from their records. This approach might be controversial, resulting in objections from more conservative community members about reintegrating potentially dangerous prisoners too quickly. An incremental, slow-go approach might help to answer these objections, since in the long run, such programs would help most ex-convicts put their lives back together and steer them

---

[267] James Kilgore, *Understanding Mass Incarceration: A People's Guide to the Key Civil Rights Struggle of Our Time*, The New Press, 2015, p. 193.

away from crime.[268] Instead of immediately providing a return of rights and a removal of information from the record, a series of milestones could be required. The milestones would require the ex-convict to accomplish certain goals to prove him or herself worthy of gaining more rights or having items removed from his or her criminal record. There might be a chart listing the things an ex-convict has to do to get points that lead to certain benefits on the way to becoming fully integrated back into the community.

A Jail Program for Drug Addicts

Another key to reducing recidivism is reducing drug addiction, which has become a fierce scourge in our nation. Rush Limbaugh's much publicized case of being addicted to pain medication drew some attention to this issue, but celebrity addicts are in a unique position. Oftentimes, they can conceal their problem with their wealth, until their addiction becomes so severe that they begin acting out of control in public.

The problem of opiate addiction which Limbaugh's case pointed to even became a campaign issue in the 2016 election. Conservative and liberal politicians alike have expressed concern about the larger problem of drugs. Conservatives have called for a crack-down on both users and the drug trade, generally involving mules bringing in drugs across the desert from Mexico. It is a battle that is still going on in the call to build a wall to keep out the "bad hombres," including drug traffickers and other criminals.

---

[268] Kerik, *From Jailer to Jailed*, p. 280.

The explosion of pain pill popping has involved individuals in all walks of life, including those in the middle and upper income brackets. It has very recently been exposed to be an outgrowth of a greedy pharmaceutical industry anxious to make profits even at the expense of human lives. This industry has been lobbying politicians to prevent regulation by the Drug Enforcement Agency.[269] The overprescribing of pain pills for all manner of physical and psychological problems has resulted in an epidemic that affects about one third of all Americans who receive pain pill prescriptions, according to recent estimates.[270] And the addiction to these expensive pain pills has caused many to resort to lower cost opiates obtained illegally, with a consequent huge rise in fatal opiate overdoses.

The vast majority of these patients have been respectable members of middle class and upper income society, so their addiction is hidden behind the leafy lawns and high priced apartments of suburbia. It is not visible on the streets, where the poor, mentally ill, and homeless addicts of hard illegal drugs congregate.

The result is that opiate addiction has become an even greater menace than addiction to crack cocaine, and less than half of the 2.2 million who need treatment receive it.[271]

---

[269] Scott Higham and Lenny Bernstein,"The Drug Industry's Triumph Over the DEA", *Washington Post*, 10/15/2017; https://www.washingtonpost.com/graphics/2017/investigations/dea-drug-industry-congress/?utm_term=.349e45a5bc19
[270] Jay Ambrose, "On to an Epidemic," *Tribune News Service*, *Arkansas Democrat-Gazette*, 3/30/17.
[271] Christine Vestal, "Still Not Enough Treatment in the Heart of the Opioid Crisis",The Pew Charitable Trusts: http://www.pewtrusts.org/en/research-and-analysis/blogs/stateline/2016/09/26/still-not-enough-treatment-in-the-heart-of-the-opioid-crisis

The opiate crisis has spread into the prisons as well, resulting in an underground network of prisoners, and even some guards, buying and selling opioids, and many of them have become addicts. Yet, some programs in prison have been found to work, such as extremely cost-effective jail treatment program in Kentucky.[272] It works because it forces addicts to confront their addiction before they hit rock bottom, when it's frequently too late, and it involves real work and commitment on the part of the inmates. The culture in this voluntary unit is very disciplined, and it successfully discourages cliques, fighting and thieving.

The program offers 12-step meetings, G.E.D. classes, exercise, meditation, prayer, counseling, writing assignments, daily work, and a re-entry program, capped off upon release with a shot of Vivitrol, which blocks the effect of opiates for a month. As a result, over half of those released remain abstinent a year later. Even though recidivism appears to have been largely unaffected, each dollar spent on the program has resulted in a savings of over four dollars.[273]

In turn, if such a program can work with extremely difficult prisoners who are deeply addicted, it provides a good model to try out in other prisons to see if the program can provide equally good results elsewhere. Any of these programs need to be monitored to show why and how they have been successful, so their success can become a model

---

[272] Sam Quinones, "A New Kind of Jail for The Opiate Age. Kentucky Is Helping Inmates Beat Addiction with Aggressive Drug Treatment," *New York Times,* 6/18/2017.
[273] Michele Staton-Tindall and Erin McNees-Winston, "Criminal Justice Kentucky Treatment Outcome Study CJKTOS", Kentucky Department of Corrections, Fiscal Year 2015; http://cdar.uky.edu/CJKTOS/Downloads/CJKTOS_FY2015_Report.pdf

for other prison officials to implement in their own institutions.

While there are also programs for at-risk juveniles, these will not be discussed here, since the juvenile justice is a separate topic that requires additional research. It is politically fraught because crime rates are highest in the 18-24 age group and almost as high among juveniles. Juveniles tend to be treated more leniently, because liberals contend their brains have not developed fully and they are subject to the stress of adolescence.

Summing Up

In summary, the main observation we have made and the changes we should make or programs we should engage in to reduce recidivism are these:

- ❖ **observations**
- ➢ **recommendations**

- ❖ Many local programs have been implemented that seem to reduce recidivism.

    - ➢ These local programs need to be promoted and then evaluated and compared on a cost-effectiveness basis to determine which are the most effective in reducing recidivism.[274]

---

[274] While I certainly agree with a recommendation for increased research on criminal justice system policies on page 11 of the National Academy book, there will be difficulties in doing such research. For one thing, it is difficult to determine how to deal with dropouts from a program when evaluating success. If the program failed to follow up on their success or

> Those programs that are the most effective should be expanded with local, state, and/or federal support.

If we can make these changes in the current status of prison management, we should be able to achieve the following:

> reduce the prison population more rapidly,

> reduce the costs of incarcerating so many prisoners,

> reduce the disintegration of black society,

> have many more ex-convicts re-enter society as productive individuals.

These developments would represent a win-win situation for all.

---

failure in re-entry into society, should the dropouts be considered program failures or ignored? In many cases the programs are too small to generate valid statistics. Finally, most of these programs rely on a combination of private donations, volunteers, and some government grants. The Law of the Jungle and the Survival of the Fittest may simply take the place of much research and evaluation.

CHAPTER 6 – MORE WAYS TO REDUCE INCARCERATION

As the previous chapters have illustrated, we can reduce recidivism by not sending technical violators of parole back to prison. But that strategy alone won't fix the problem. It is likely that several different solutions have to be imposed to fix our massive problem of over-incarceration. Before proposing all sorts of possible solutions, we should consider two things:

1) Who is in the best position to correct the problem without significant increases in costs.

2) What factors might contribute to or limit any practical implementation of such proposed solutions.

Then, we can select the approaches that should be the most effective in reducing incarceration.

Should the Feds Take the Lead or States and Counties?

Given these problems of over-incarceration in both state and federal prisons, the next question is what to do about it, and what is the best level of government to lead this effort. In general, the states should lead the charge.

The reason the states should take the lead is because state prisons with their larger prison population account for the vast majority of the increase in incarceration. The states need to take the lead in reducing incarceration, particularly if criminal justice reform is not a federal priority. Their action is particular needed now under the Trump administration and as long as partisan political gridlock continues in Washington.

Since most prisoners are in state prisons, states are footing the bill for most prisoners right now, as well as spending more on other correction strategies -- far outpacing what the federal government spends. These patterns are illustrated in the chart on page 21, which shows how much more incarceration occurs in state prisons than federal ones, costing states much more than the federal government. [275]

The Role Conservatives Can Play in Fixing the System

As the foregoing discussion has shown, local conservatives are in an increasingly powerful position to take the lead in fixing the criminal justice system, including reducing unnecessary incarcerations and the excess costs associated with them. In the South and Midwest, conservatives control state governments. Moreover, a growing national leadership, supported by the conservative media, is contributing to this growing strength of the movement. So conservatives take heart!

This growing national leadership includes such powerful figures in politics, industry, and the media as Newt Gingrich, Grover Nordquist, the lobbyist who has conservative congressmen sign pledges to support no new taxes, the Koch brothers, Rand Paul, and the libertarian Cato Institute. These conservatives, plus many others, have been offering their public support for efforts to fix the criminal justice system with a view toward making it operate more efficiently and at a lower cost. For example, in 2010, Gingrich and former California legislator Pat Nolan published

---

[275] Jeremy Travis, Bruce Western and Steve Redburn, Editors, *The Growth of Incarceration in the United States: Exploring Causes and Consequences*, National Academies Press, 2014, Figure 11-1

an op-ed in the *Washington Post* stating that "the criminal justice system is broken and conservatives must lead the way in fixing it." Conservatives have also publicly endorsed the use of faith-based initiatives to turn around the lives of convicted criminals who have previously been deemed incorrigible.

These new conservative voices supporting criminal justice reform represent a major change, since this growing movement enables conservatives to take the lead in shaping the national agenda and proposing conservative solutions to what has long been a costly, seemingly insoluble problem. In the past, the issue of crime reduction has been regarded by the general public and media as an issue "owned" by liberals,[276] whose approach to most crime problems has been to advocate fewer laws and lesser penalties for crime. In other words, their approach has been to tamp down the definition of what is a crime or a criminal in the interest of fewer penalties, consistent with their popular designation as "bleeding hearts."

The Effectiveness of the Conservative Approach in the South

A conservative approach can work well in the South, which has the highest incarceration rates of any region of the country and is solidly red. As a result, the South is an ideal incubator for instituting the new conservative remedies, since reforms can be implemented with few concessions and little liberal opposition. This has already been the case in Texas starting in 2007, in Georgia in 2014 and in Mississippi.[277]

---

[276] Dagan and Telles, *Prison Break*, Oxford University Press, 2016.
[277] Ibid.

By concentrating on rehabilitation and outcomes, Texas diverted those with drug addictions to treatment programs with weekly random drug tests, reduced the number of parolees sent back to prison for technical violations by 39%, and saved $2 billion.[278] This diversion program may not have reduced incarcerations, but it stopped the increases, avoided the need for building more prisons,[279] indeed even closing three.[280]

Georgia undertook reforms which facilitated access to stable housing and finding employment.[281] Sentence lengths were reduced for most offenses, and prison commitments fell by13%. The state managed to reduce its prison population from 54,895 to 52,962, which avoided estimated increases of $264 million for additional prisons.[282]

Mississippi managed to drop from the nation's second highest imprisonment rate to the fifth highest, avoiding estimated increases of $266 million for additional prisons. It reduced imprisonments for technical violations of parole, thereby increasing the proportion of prisoners convicted of violent crimes from 46% to 56%.[283]

---

[278] Rick Perry, Former Governor of Texas, "Follow the Texas Model", Brennan Center for Justice, 4/27/15

[279] Caitlin Dunklee and Rebecca Larsen, "Setting the Record Straight on Texas "Prison Reform", *UT News, The University of Texas at Austin,* 8/10/2015.

[280] Scott Henson, "What's Next for Texas criminal justice reform?", *Texas Observer*, 3/21/2016.

[281] MIchael P. Boggs and W. Thomas Worthy, "Report of the Georgia Council on Criminal Justice Reform", State of Georgia, January, 2014.

[282] Elizabeth Pelletier, Bryce Peterson and Ryan King, "Assessing the Impact of Georgia's Sentencing Reforms", Justice Policy Notes, Urban Institute, July, 2017

[283] Grover Nordquist, "Nation Taking Notice of Mississippi Prison Reform," *Clarion Ledger*, 4/9/2016.

A similar conservative reform approach is happening in Arkansas. The state recently passed The Criminal Justice Efficiency and Safety Act legislation,[284] which provides for the following policy changes to reduce incarceration:

- Parolees and probationers will experience swift and certain sanctioning for minor violations of parole or probation by receiving 45-180 day sentences in Arkansas Community Correction facilities instead of going to prison. In turn, this reduction in time in prison might free up 1600 prison beds and save over $30 million. [285,286,287]

- Ex-cons who are experiencing a mental health crisis or are found to be high on drugs will be diverted to one of three planned Crisis Stabilization units to receive up to 10 days of treatment. They will also receive a subsequent possible long-term commitment to a residential facility instead of going back to jail or prison.[288,289] One estimate has suggested that mentally ill prisoners incur costs that are 20-25 times more than outside treatment, and that the costs of imprisoning the mentally ill could be eating up nearly half the state's

---

[284] Summarized earlier on pages 142-145.

[285] Lindsey Millar, "Criminal Justice: Actual Reform," *Arkansas Times*, 4/13/2017.

[286] John Moritz, "Prison Board Oks Plan For Parole, Probation Violators," *Arkansas Democrat-Gazette*, 6/27/2017.

[287] John Moritz, "New Law Provides Sidetrack to Prison," *Arkansas Democrat-Gazette*, 10/1/2017.

[288] Lindsey Millar, "Criminal Justice: Actual Reform," *Arkansas Times*, 4/13/2017.

[289] Brandon Mulder, "6 Counties Vie to Be Selected for Crisis Units. Centers to Take Mentally Ill Otherwise Bound for Jail Cell," *Arkansas Democrat-Gazette*, 6/28/2017.

budget for its Department of Corrections.[290] However, the fact that the Crisis Stabilization Units will have very few beds reserved for short term treatment[291] indicates that follow-up treatment may require much more significant attention.

- Funds saved from these approaches could easily have been used up by an Arkansas Senate bill aimed at longer sentencing for repeat offenders, estimated to add about 5500 more prisoners over 10 years at a cost of nearly $700 million.[292] Fortunately for taxpayers, this bill was not passed by the Arkansas House or signed into law.[293]
- Another recent suggestion has been made to reduce the occupational licensing requirements that serve as high barriers for ex-offenders seeking employment. This approach would incur hardly any costs at all.[294]

These cost-saving approaches make much more sense for reforming the system than the efforts of liberals who are

---

[290] "A Brief Cost Analysis of Arkansas Mental Health and Prison Reform", Arkansas Public Policy Panel, April, 2015; https://static1.squarespace.com/static/55afb880e4b039b081c51cbc/t/55ba30fae4b0b0462f40a157/1438265594437/Mental+Health+Report.pdf

[291] Arkansas is now anticipated to have 4 such units, but the first one in our most populous county will have only 16 beds: Emma Pettit, "County identifies site, medical provider for mental health Crisis Center", *Arkansas Democrat-Gazette*, 11/22/2017.

[292] Brian Fanney and John Moritz, "Senate Backs Longer Prison Stays for Repeat Offenders," *Arkansas Democrat-Gazette*, 3/23/2017.

[293] Bryan B. King, "Arkansas Senate Bill SB 177: Requiring a Person Who Has Three or More Previous Commitments to the Department of Corrections to Serve at Least Eighty Percent of His or Her Sentence for His or Her Next Commitment to the Department Before Being Eligible for Parole"; https://openstates.org/ar/bills/2017/SB177

[294] Thomas Snyder and Alexandria Tatem, "To Reduce Crime. State Has Means, Without Cost," *Arkansas Democrat-Gazette*, 9/28/2017.

intent on placating black and Hispanic minorities in blue states. As a result, blue states are running up the tab for their excesses, which are now expected to exceed $75,000 per inmate in California[295] and over $150,000 per inmate on Rikers Island in New York.[296] That's many times what we pay to incarcerate inmates in the South. Unfortunately, these high costs will also affect conservative taxpayers in the blue states, since they don't have the power there to gain sufficient support to pass more conservative measures. So all conservatives there can do is agree with their liberal counterparts that criminal justice reform is needed and not try to block their efforts, unless these liberal policies seek to heap further burdens on taxpayers in those blue states. Perhaps then conservatives might a least be able to block such measures from passing or negotiate keeping the budgets for these new liberal programs down.

　　　States that have legislatures which are more evenly divided between Republicans and Democrats may be likely to have the most difficult time because of partisan infighting and a battle over who gets the credit for advancing this issue. An example of such infighting led to the political demise of conservative Democratic Senator Jim Webb from Virginia, after he issued a call for national criminal justice reform. But he narrowly failed to generate a successful bipartisan coalition, and then he lost re-election. His call for national reform might have fared better if he had been a Republican. Then, he could have been in a better position to gain support from conservatives, who make up the main contingent of voters in the Republican Party.

---

[295] Don Thompson, "California Per-Inmate Cost to Hit Record,"*Associated Press, Arkansas Democrat-Gazette*, 6/5/2017.
[296] Partly due to failing to close some of their facilities while the number of inmates has declined

Yet, regardless of the outcome in particular races, conservative values are gaining support nationally, as reflected in the takeover by Republicans of a majority of both Houses of Congress, as well as the Presidency. Although conservatives and liberal/progressives approach solving the problems in the criminal justice system with different values and strategies, both can agree on the bedrock principle of the conservative approach -- that we are incarcerating too many prisoners at too great a cost. Certainly Bernard Kerik supports bipartisan efforts.[297] Liberals come from the perspective that these changes must be made to reduce the suffering of those convicted. Conservatives are more concerned with the need for law and order and restitution to help the victims. Yet both sides do want the system to be more effective and cost less.

Given these commonalities in goals, despite different ideas for achieving them, it seems likely that both sides will eventually find a way to work together to find solutions in a bipartisan fashion and gain credit from the public for achieving these goals. Doing so will help to concurrently increase rehabilitation, reduce recidivism, reduce unnecessary and costly incarceration, and lead to less crime.

Incentives for Increasing or Decreasing Incarcerations

A big problem in deciding what to do to reduce incarceration is that there are incentives for both increasing it and decreasing it. What are these conflicting pressures? That's what I want to discuss next.

---

[297] Kerik, *From Jailer to Jailed*, p.244.

Incentives for Increasing Incarceration

Keeping the public safe from criminals is the primary incentive for increasing incarcerations. This pressure to lock 'em up is fed by fear, and the local news constantly trumpets the latest crimes. That keeps people afraid, even though statistics may present a very different picture. The reality is that the crime rate[298] is actually decreasing for most crimes. But the media makes it seem like there is a criminal lurking on every corner -- so better lock 'em to be safe and not sorry.

Given the widespread fear of crime, juiced by the media, it's no wonder that politicians and elected prosecutors respond with a law and order approach. Another reason that politicians and prosecutors argue for more incarcerations is that the political cost of making a misjudgment to release a criminal who then commits a heinous crime is very high.[299] This is exemplified by the defeat of Michael Dukakis in the

---

[298] Crimes per capita or per 100,000 persons
[299] Pfaff, *Locked In*, 2017, pp. 140, 168, 224.

1988 presidential campaign, primarily attributed to his pardoning of Willie Horton - a misstep repeatedly reinforced in campaign ads against Dukakis.

How the Census Promotes Longer Sentences

Another incentive for increasing incarceration is the way representation for voting is assigned by the census. It turns out that it is better to have more prisoners. The census rolls work this way because currently prisoners are considered residents of the county where the prison is located, although they cannot vote. Consequently, counties with prisons have an incentive to lock up more prisoners, because that increases the census count. In this way, their voting citizens gain greater representation due to the county's higher census count.[300]

Incentives for Decreasing Incarceration

By comparison, cost savings is the primary incentive for decreasing incarceration, especially for conservatives.

In contrast, liberals don't advocate either argument - saving money by reducing incarceration or increasing safety by increasing incarceration. Instead, their position is in favor of reducing incarceration in order to reduce the disproportionate incarceration of minorities.

It is as if the two sides -- conservatives and liberals are talking past each other, because they have different reasons for supporting either reducing or increasing incarceration -- and their arguments are not necessarily driven by the facts but

---

[300] Pfaff, *Locked In,* 2017, p. 173.

by their emotions and preconceptions of what has what effect on what, even if their view is at odds with the actual facts.

In any event, liberals have a less convincing argument, so they have less control over the situation than conservatives. This state of affairs occurs because, according to social psychologists, more people respond from fear in looking out for themselves and their families to stay safe than out of concern for strangers, such as innocent victims who may be unfairly incarcerated. Moreover, the political cost of locking up even several innocent people appears to be quite small relative to the cost of making one mistake by releasing a parolee who goes on to commit another crime.[301]

Under the circumstances, reducing the influence of elected officials on the process of making decisions about the everyday operations of the correctional systems might help reduce incarceration. Pfaff suggests appointing prosecutors and judges so as to shield political officials from the influence of the public,[302] since under the influence of the media, the public perceives that crime is always rising, even when it is really falling.[303] Thus, incentives to decrease incarceration must reduce incentives for prosecutors in order to increase incarceration.

For example, another prosecutor-related incentive for increasing incarceration is that the vast majority of prosecutors are county prosecutors, and they send more prisoners to state prisons than to county jails. Consequently, the counties who pay the prosecutors don't have to foot the bill for the prosecutors' actions, and the prosecutors feel no consequences for locking up more people. Instead, the states

---

[301] Pfaff, *Locked In*, 2017, pp. 168-171.
[302] Ibid., pp. 161, 182, 217.
[303] Ibid., p. 169.

pay for the incarceration, though they have little control or oversight over the process.[304]

Measures to be Considered

Now let's turn to proposed measures to decrease incarceration without endangering public safety, emphasizing those measures that can be accomplished without large increases in cost.

Why Longer Sentences Aren't a Deterrent

Despite the push for longer sentences to combat crime by keeping criminals off the streets, this approach is ineffective for certain types of crimes, because incarceration may not be much more of a deterrent with longer sentences than with shorter ones. Most youthful offenders simply do not take the potential for going to prison into account when they impulsively commit a violent crime.

Longer incarceration is also a less effective deterrent to crime than the certainty of punishment.[305] Unfortunately, the prospect for punishment is not at all certain, since the police only solve about two thirds of murders and about half of aggravated assault cases. And the likelihood of solving the case is even less for property crimes, since the police only solve 13-14% of burglaries and auto thefts. On the other hand, when individuals are tested for drugs and immediately penalized with not too severe sanctions, there is a greater reduction in recidivism.

---

[304] Ibid., pp. 163-166.
[305] Pfaff, *Locked In*, 2017, pp. 194-196.

For example, that's what happened for "Swift, Certain and Fair," an around-the-country outgrowth of Hawaii's Opportunity Probation with Enforcement (HOPE) program. HOPE tests for drugs daily and imposes immediate short term jail sanctions of a few days, that are not too severe, resulting in improved outcomes. After one year, only 21% of participants in the HOPE program were rearrested compared to 47% of non-participants, were incarcerated only about half as many days, and had a radically lower rate of positive drug testing, 13% vs. 46%.[306,307]

Juveniles Should Not Be Imprisoned Together with Seasoned Adult Criminals

Long-time Republican law and order advocate Bernard Kerik points to the dangers of long sentences with youthful offenders. As he asserts: "If we do not shorten their sentences….we may as well sentence them to life in prison or death."[308] The reason for this outcome is that a long-term prison sentence exposes the juvenile offender to a virtual school for crime, as he or she learns different crime techniques from seasoned criminals who serve as mentors.

---

[306] "Hawaii's Opportunity Probation with Enforcement (HOPE) Program", Coalition for Evidence-Based Policy Newsletter Summary, 2/2011; http://evidencebasedprograms.org/wp-content/uploads/2012/12/HOPE-Program-Feb-2011.pdf
[307] "Swift, Certain, and Fair (SCF) Supervision Program – Including Project HOPE FY 2017 Competitive Grant Announcement", U.S. Department of Justice ,Office of Justice Programs, Bureau of Justice Assistance,1/19/2017; https://www.bja.gov/funding/SCF17.pdf
[308] Kerik, *From Jailer to Jailed*, p. 262.

Reducing the Number and Length of Incarcerations

Alternatives to prison, such as probation, electronic monitoring, substance abuse and mental health treatment, community service, and fines, should all be more seriously considered in cases of nonviolent crimes. These are all ways to reduce the costs of unnecessary imprisonment, as well as help to increase family stability and help the ex-convict become a contributing and productive member of society.

As pointed out in *American Justice?,* we shouldn't imprison people for nonviolent small quantity drug offenses. Not only is this imprisonment expensive and reduces the individual's contribution of productive labor, but this lock 'em up approach doesn't win the War on Drugs, because other users and dealers take their place. Such imprisonment only overcrowds our prisons and costs too much. Not only are too many people being incarcerated, but their sentences have grown too long, increasing on average by 33% between 1993 and 2009. [309]

One approach is to shorten sentences for certain crimes. As the National Academy book *The Growth of Incarceration in the United States: Exploring Causes and Consequences*, stated:

> "RECOMMENDATION: Given the small crime prevention effects of long prison sentences and the possibly high financial, social, and human costs of incarceration, federal and state policy makers should revise current criminal justice policies to significantly reduce the rate of incarceration in the United States. In

---

[309] Lauren-Brooke Eisen and Inimai Chettiar, "39% of Prisoners Should Not Be in Prison," *Time,* 12/8/2016, http://time.com/4596081/incarceration-report

particular, they should reexamine policies regarding mandatory prison sentences and long sentences. Policy makers should also take steps to improve the experience of incarcerated men and women and reduce unnecessary harm to their families and their communities."[310]

As previously discussed, the high numbers of prisoners and their long sentences wreak havoc on families. After release, the prior imprisonment also contributes to unemployment and underemployment, since having a prison record makes it more difficult to get a job. High incarceration rates and lengths of prison sentences are financially costly for society, too.

Thus, to reduce these economic and social costs, the Brennan Center recommends a 25% reduction in prison sentence lengths for nonviolent crimes. To illustrate the cost savings for a small reduction in the prison population, the Brennan Center estimated that such a 25% reduction in sentence length would reduce the approximately 1.5 million prison population by 212,000 (14%) and save $6.6 billion annually. The Urban Institute similarly estimated that a 25% reduction in sentence length by itself would cause a 15% total decline in the prison population by 2021.[311]

Perhaps this reduction should be even larger in order to save even more money, since a 25% reduction in sentence length would still not restore prison sentence lengths to the shorter levels that were present in 1993, just after violent crime had peaked nationally. One way to save even more would be to additionally reduce the number of prisoners as

------

[310]Jeremy Travis, Bruce Western, and Steve Redburn, Editors, *The Growth of Incarceration in the United States: Exploring Causes and Consequences*, National Academies Press, 2014, p. 9.
[311] Pfaff, *Locked In*, 2017, pp. 64-65.

well as their sentences. For example, the Brennan Center estimated that if the 25% reduction in sentence length were accompanied by a proposed 25% reduction in prisoners, the annual savings are estimated to be over $18 billion.[312] This reduction in prisoners could be readily accomplished by making lower level nonviolent crimes not punishable by imprisonment.

Still another way to reduce incarcerations for non-violent prisoners is to tie a reduction in a sentence to participation in skills training or getting an educational degree. The advantage here is giving the individual convicted of a crime an opportunity to learn better job skills that can lead to employment outside of prison and a decline in subsequent criminality. This is an approach that was implemented by corrections officials in California. In March 2017, they announced that they would implement new sentencing rules that would allow inmates to qualify for reduced sentences, if they earned a college degree or participated in self-help programs. Even though police and prosecutors objected to the program, the corrections officials went ahead with the program, since they estimated these reduced sentences would trim California's prison population by 9500 over four years,[313] with a predicted savings of $23 million in its first year.[314] A reduction of 9500 is only about one-third the number of prison inmates moved to county jails or parole a few years earlier, which resulted in a 17% drop in

---

[312] "Unnecessarily Incarcerated," Brennan Center, https://www.brennancenter.org/sites/default/files/publications/Unnecessarily_Incarcerated.pdf

[313] "New California rules to cut prison terms", *Compiled by Arkansas Democrat-Gazette Staff from wire reports, Arkansas Democrat-Gazette*, 3/25/2017.

[314] "The 2017-18 Budget. Implementation of Proposition 57", LAO Report, 4/6/2017; http://www.lao.ca.gov/Publications/Report/3648

their prison population with no significant increase in crime.[315] While 9500 is a relatively small number, it might be regarded as a good first step to show that this program works and thereby allay the concerns of police and prosecutors who have visions of criminals escaping from what they consider a just punishment. If the sentence reduction works to reduce costs and crime, redirecting ex-cons into productive work instead of returning to crime and more prison time, it would represent a worthwhile tactic to reduce incarceration.

Another Initial Fix to Reduce Incarceration

The liberal approach to simply release more prisoners would yield only temporary results because of recidivism. The Brennan Center for Justice has estimated that 39% of the prison population could be released without significantly impacting public safety.[316] The Center claims this release is justified because some of the crimes were so minor and non-violent that they should not have led to incarceration in the first place (25%) or because the time already served by the prisoner would constitute a just sentence (14%).

The effect of the Brennan Center proposal on the number of imprisoned inmates is shown below, though a 39% reduction would not suffice to fix the situation. That's because most of the 39% released will probably become recidivists unless something else is done to address that. As

---

[315] Tom Jackman, "Mass Reduction of California Prison Population Didn't Cause Rise in Crime, Two Studies Find." *Washington Post* 5/18/2016.
[316] "Unnecessarily Incarcerated," Brennan Center, https://www.brennancenter.org/sites/default/files/publications/Unnecessa rily_Incarcerated.pdf

illustrated in the chart below, the intent of the Brennan Center proposal is to rapidly and permanently reduce the prison population (filled squares, labeled as originally envisaged). However, the reduction isn't maintained when you take recidivism into account. Without any supplemental programs, the drop in imprisonment is only about half as much, *and the reduction is not maintained* (partially filled squares). On the other hand, if you simultaneously reduce recidivism by 33% by eliminating imprisonment for technical violations of parole, then the reduction in imprisonment (open triangles) is much greater and maintained much longer.

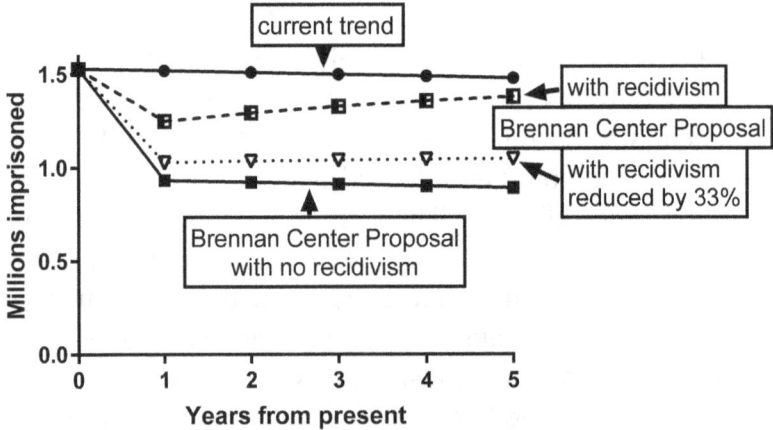

Another problem with simply releasing prisoners is that a 39% release of prisoners would certainly be too drastic. Both law and order proponents and the general public would legitimately fear releasing so many criminals at one time, particularly without adequate rehabilitation, because many would likely commit new crimes.

On top of that, most don't realize that almost 42% of all prisoners are released annually already, but 55% of them wind up back in prison due to recidivism, where they join new inmates who number about the same as the other 45% of those released. So the numbers in prison ultimately remain the same.[317]

Do those liberals really think we should release 39% of the prisoners on top of the 42% already being released? That would mean releasing 39 + 42 = 81% of all our prisoners in one year! Will they next ask us to just open the prison doors and release all of them? Do they expect to release prisoners with no retraining for re-entry? And won't 55% of the prisoners be back within a year?

Accordingly, like many others who suggest a gradual introduction of reforms, I recommend that any release be delayed a year to permit sufficient rehabilitation training for those to be released. I also recommend that approximately 10% of the inmates be released each year over the next four years, which will eventually accomplish the 39% release, only more gradually, as illustrated on the chart below.

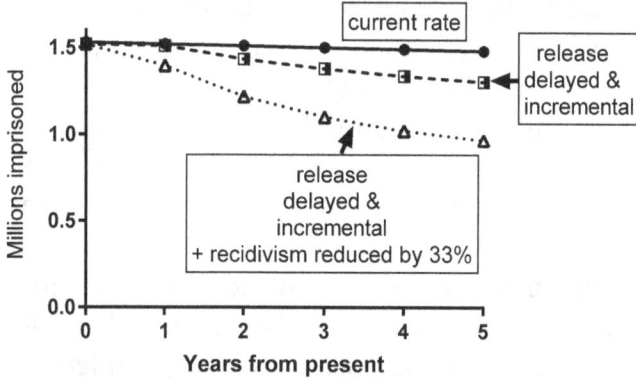

Because of the high rate of recidivism, the prison population will still be over 1.3 million at the end of five years (release delayed & incremental). But if this is accompanied by a 33% reduction in recidivism by not

---

[317] "3 in 4 Former Prisoners in 30 States Arrested Within 5 Years of Release", Office of Justice Programs, Bureau of Justice Statistics, 4/22/2014; https://www.bjs.gov/content/pub/press/rprts05p0510pr.cfm

imprisoning technical violators of parole,[318] the number of prisoners would drop to around 965,000 (dotted line).

Again we see the reducing recidivism is key to making any dent in the prison population. This reduction occurred merely by not imprisoning technical violators of parole. Consider that it may be possible to generate an even greater than 33% reduction in recidivism, if effective re-entry programs steer ex-convicts into productive work by giving them the necessary job skills and support to return to the workforce.

Dealing with Violent Criminals

While decriminalizing drugs and shortening sentences alone may reduce our incarceration problem, it won't solve it.[319] As Pfaff indicates in *Locked In*, half of all those in state prisons have been convicted of violent crimes, and these convicts should not be released. Indeed, the proportion of inmates in prisons convicted of violent crimes increased from 36% in the 1980s to 60% since the 1990s.[320]

To deal with this hardened criminal element, Pfaff suggests that the estimated $20 billion savings from diverting non-violent criminals outside of the prison system into other programs could be reinvested into different strategies to reduce crime further. For example, the police and probation departments, which are under local and state jurisdiction, could hire 270,000 new police officers or 360,000 probation

---

[318] Some of the alternatives to imprisonment of technical violators of parole might include probation, electronic monitoring, treatment for drug abuse and mental health, community service, and fines and restitution.
[319] Pfaff, *Locked In*, 2017, p. 6.
[320] Ibid., 2017, pp. 33, 187.

officers. Some of the savings could be used to reduce state budgets.[321]

However, savings may not be so large, because prisons and jails will still need to be operated, even with reduced numbers of inmates. And because of the increase in violent criminals, these facilities can't be closed entirely, so any savings may only be one-third as much as the Brennan Center projected.[322] Even so, it will certainly be helpful to reduce costs some and increase the chances for reduced recidivism with various re-rentry support programs to help ex-cons get productive work and integrate back into the community.

While this is significant progress, other measures could reduce incarceration further, as described next.

Measures Requiring More Time to Reduce Incarceration

While reducing recidivism and releasing less dangerous prisoners in tandem may lead to significant reduction in incarceration within five years, additional approaches could lead to even greater reductions. Some of these approaches would require more legislation and/or more time to be implemented. Consequently, they need to be started soon in order to implement them and assess the results over the next few years. Then, the most effective approaches could be determined, continued, and even expanded to result in further reductions in incarcerations and costs.

---

[321] "Unnecessarily Incarcerated," Brennan Center, https://www.brennancenter.org/sites/default/files/publications/Unnecessarily_Incarcerated.pdf
[322] Pfaff, *Locked In*, 2017, p. 99.

Accordingly, I would begin by supporting criminologist John Pfaff's recommendations:

> ➤ Greater funds should be provided for indigent defense attorneys, so they are not so badly outclassed by prosecutors.[323] Providing these finds is needed, since 80% of people charged with crimes cannot afford a defense attorney, and they aren't provided with an adequate defense by beleaguered public defenders.[324] A good reason for improving their defense abilities is that 95% of defendants end up taking a plea deal. Many admit to crimes they are not responsible for committing. With a better defense, many defendants accused of non-violent crimes could be guided into rehabilitative programs that would reduce their likelihood of engaging in criminal activity again.

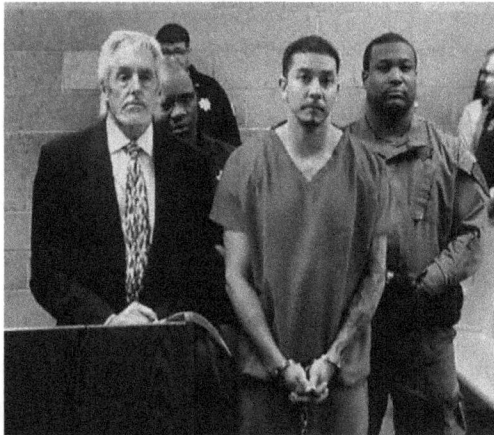

> ➤ Expand the Justice Reinvestment Initiative from its current 31 states to the rest of the country. This

---

[323] Pfaff, *Locked In*, 2017, pp. 137, 154-156, 207.
[324] James Forman, Jr., "Justice Springs Eternal", *New York Times*, 3/25/17

initiative aims to increase the efficiency of dollars spent on the correctional system and give us the most bang for our bucks. It will divert money from prisons to effective alternatives to incarceration and allow funds to be transferred from state to county and county to city.[325]

> Set up sentencing commissions, currently in 21 states, in other states, and encourage these commissions to work together to create a uniform set of sentencing guidelines for each state. These commissions should be composed of prosecutors, judges, legislators, defense attorneys, academics, and even former inmates and victims. They should be tasked with gathering research on the most current studies on the effectiveness of different sentencing practices. Then, armed with this knowledge, the commissions should exert considerable influence over how sentencing laws are written and implemented.[326]

In addition to the above recommendations made by Pfaff, I recommend the following:

> Establish addiction treatment centers in major cities, since treatment at these centers is likely to result in the successful reentry of many former addicts back into society. These centers would be staffed by a team of psychologists, social workers, and medical professionals with an expertise in addiction problems. Ex-convicts with addictions would be required to go to regular support group meetings, along with individual

---

[325] Pfaff, *Locked In*, 2017, p. 226.
[326] Pfaff, *Locked In*, 2017, p. 221.

meetings with an assigned counselor. Such ex-convicts would also be regularly monitored through urine testing protocols, in order to determine if the program is working for them. If not, additional treatment modalities might be added. While the costs of such treatment might seem high, the ex-con addict would probably only require treatment for a few months, resulting in major long-term savings. The program would not need to be extended beyond a few months for those who are not helped.

Longer Term Approaches to Reduce Incarcerations

Besides the initial strategies previously suggested and those requiring more time to implement, some still longer term approaches may also reduce incarcerations and costs. One approach is to provide different incentives to private prisons to encourage them to make changes in the prison, so that it participates in the rehabilitative effort to keep prisoners from coming back after they are released. Pfaff made the following recommendation:

> ➢ Incentivize private prisons by paying them based on how their prisoners perform after release. This would be similar to suggestions to improve healthcare by incentivizing medical groups to pay for improved health outcomes for their patients, rather than allowing them to charge fees for each service rendered. Currently prisons are paid based on how many prisoners they house, and if a former prisoner returns, the private prison profits.[327] Private prisons can

---

[327] Pfaff, *Locked In*, 2017, p. 224.

respond much more quickly to mandates or incentives to make changes, whereas public prisons depend on the passage of legislation or some public approval process, which could be difficult in these divisive times. Therefore, it would make more sense to enroll private prisons in efforts to give prisoners the tools they need to better readjust when they are released.

Additionally, I recommend the following policy change:

➤ Mentally ill prisoners could be reduced through early releases, probably into something resembling halfway houses with properly trained staff. This early release could significantly reduce prison costs, since so many mentally ill persons are in prison. It may be worthwhile to consider re-establishing psychiatric hospitals that would represent a more humane alternative to prisons. Such large facilities might produce an economy of scale, but it will take years to establish such a system.

Finally, I agree with Pfaff's argument that prosecutors need to be held more accountable for their actions because they have too much power and not enough accountability. They have so much power, because 95% of cases are decided by plea bargains, which for the most part are dictated by prosecutors, rather than judges.

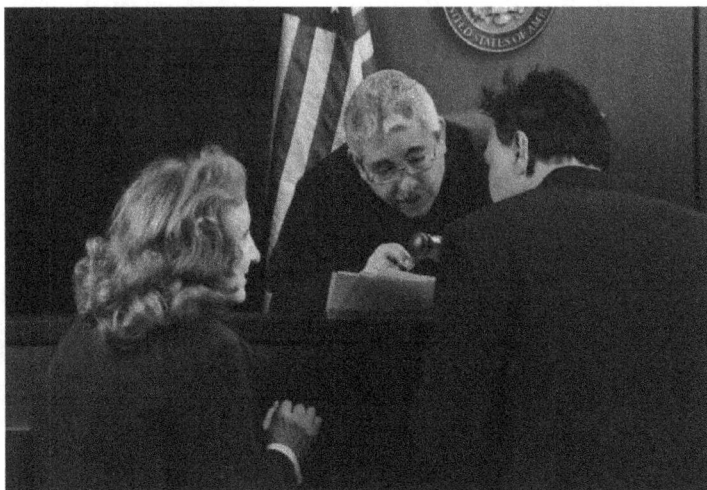

Most of the cases involve indigent arrestees who are assigned defense lawyers, who have neither the time nor the resources to prepare a proper defense.[328] For example, over a four year period, one public defender dealt with 1400 cases but only 14 went to trial.[329] Under the circumstances, I agree with the following recommendations by Pfaff:

➢ Prosecutors should be appointed rather than elected, because that would diminish the influence of demands of the public for public safety, which has led to over-incarceration.[330]

➢ Different sets of prosecutors should serve urban and suburban areas, so the prosecutors are more responsive

---

[328] Pfaff, *Locked In*, 2017, p. 132.
[329] Marc Lamont Hill, *Nobody: Casualties of America's War on the Vulnerable, from Ferguson to Flint and Beyond*, Atria Books, 2017, p. 78.
[330] Pfaff, *Locked In*, 2017, p. 217.

to the characteristics and needs of those areas with their different populations. Suburban citizens are not particularly aware of the difficulties that minorities in higher crime urban ghettos face.[331] Thus, just as it is best to look for local solutions for local problems, it is better to seek to hire prosecutors who are more attuned to local conditions.[332]

> A financial realignment should be made to shift imprisonment costs to the counties that pay prosecutors, making them more financially responsible. Prosecutors currently are under no pressure to keep costs down, because states foot the bill for the prisoners that prosecutors convict. If necessary, this new policy could require each county to be assigned a cap on the number of inmates it could send to state prisons, with any county having to buy prison "beds" from other counties if they exceed their cap.[333]

> New sentencing and plea bargain guidelines should be established to reduce the number of years in a sentence for non-violent crimes. These guidelines should also reduce the pressures on poor defendants to plead guilty in cases where they fear the risks of a much longer, harsher sentence, if they go to trial represented by a public defender overloaded with cases.[334] Making

---

[331] Pfaff, *Locked In*, 2017, pp. 213-215.

[332] In *American Justice?*, I previously made a similar suggestion that separate court systems should be set up for urban and suburban/rural districts within counties.

[333] Pfaff, *Locked In*, 2017, pp. 163-166, 210-211.

[334] Ibid, pp. 199, 210-211

these worthwhile changes in sentencing and plea bargain guidelines will take a long time to accomplish, given the need for extensive hearings and public discussion of any major policy changes in the criminal justice system.

➤ Future census counts should assign prisoners to the counties where they resided before they were imprisoned. This will enable better tracking of the results of new policy interventions.

A Fix to Reduce the Numbers of Arrestees in Jail

In addition to reducing the numbers of inmates in prisons, attempts should be made to reduce the numbers of defendants in jails. It is critical to also reduce the 630,000 people in jails, both to reduce costs and the injustices to those who are in jail, because they cannot afford the cost of making bail and may be innocent.

This jail population is a very different population serving a much shorter amount of time than prisoners, since jail terms are only for up to 1 year for less serious crimes. Additionally, jails serve as a holding center for many defendants who have not even been sentenced and might be judged not guilty once they finally get their day in court.

Under the circumstances, a large percentage of these defendants don't need to be in jail and could be safely released. Their release would result in considerable cost savings to the cities, counties and states where they are housed. Criminal justice researchers estimate that 83% of all

people in jail are there because they can't afford bail.[335]
Often they are there because of local conflicts, such as a one-
time domestic disturbances or fights and are not a risk for
offending again. Most of them are not flight risks because,
unlike white collar criminals, they cannot afford to leave
home because of their limited funds, which is why they can't
afford to make bail in the first place, even for a minor
offense.[336]

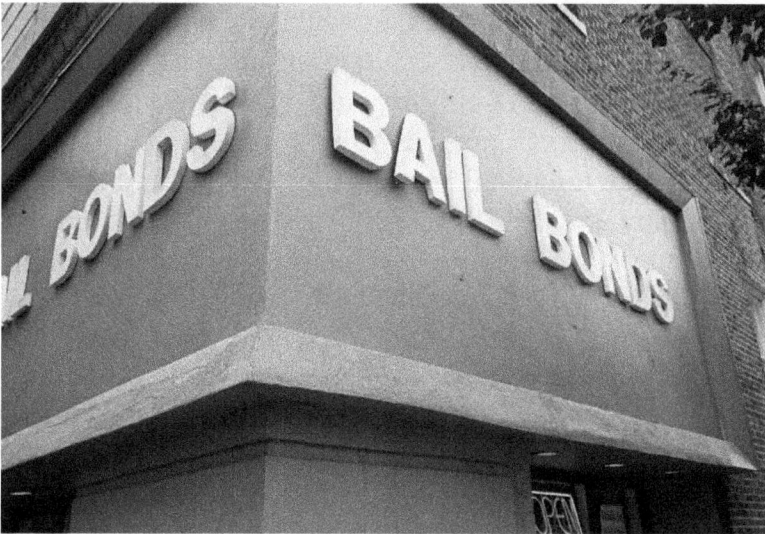

Thus, a key change that is needed to keep defendants
with less serious charges out of jail is fixing the bail bond
requirements. Ostensibly, these requirements are designed to
help defendants by giving them the money they need to stay
out of jail while their case proceeds through the system. But,
in fact, it exploits the requirement for bail by setting

---

[335] Marc Lamont Hill, *Nobody*, p. 65.
[336] Ginia Bellafante, "Petty Crimes, Daunting Bail: Next Step in Criminal
Justice Reform", *New York Times*, 6/4/2017.

exorbitant fees that low-income defendants can't afford without getting funds from their families and friends, who end up paying typically 10% of the total bail. Here's how the system works.

Bail bonds currently represent a for-profit industry that is only found in the U.S. and the Philippines.[337] Bail bond policy costs arrestees, primarily poor ones, 14 billion dollars a year by throwing them in jail. The vast majority of arrestees cannot afford to post bond themselves. Bail bonds represent a contract with bail bondsmen, in which the bail paid cannot be recovered and is frequently paid in installments with interest amounting to $1.4-2.4 billion annually.[338] A portion of the profit goes to a small number of bail insurance corporations.

Remaining in jail because they can't afford to post bail causes many arrestees to accept plea deals just to end their in limbo status while waiting for their day in court, even if they were innocent. The acceptance of these plea deals and the negative consequences of accepting them are reflected in increased conviction rates for those who can't afford bail versus those who can. Accordingly, the conviction rates in New York City for those who didn't make bail were 92%, compared to only 50% for those who were bailed out.[339]

High bonds are unnecessary or excessive for low-income defendants with less serious non-violent crimes, because most of these bonds are for people at low flight risk, many of whose charges will be dropped. The cost to the justice system, communities, and individuals has been estimated to be as much as 10 times higher than the $14

---

[337] ACLU Campaign for Smart Justice, "Selling off Our Freedom: How Insurance Corporations Have Taken Over Our Bail System", May 2017, p. 2.
[338] Ibid., p. 9.
[339] Ibid., p. 18

billion in direct payments.[340] A substantial part of these sums could be saved by:

> Reforming the bail bond system by returning to the 1966 Bail Reform Act which requires using the least restrictive lower bail approach to ensure an arrestee shows up in court rather than confining him in jail.[341] This would be a more reasonable and cost-effective approach in that over 60% of those in jail have not been convicted and are in pretrial detention.[342] Such an approach would certainly reduce the numbers of arrestees in jail, though it would not have much impact on the prison population.

> Abolishing for-profit bail, an approach already carried out in New Jersey, Illinois, Kentucky, and Oregon.[343] These states and others, as well as federal courts, use pretrial risk assessment to determine who to release on

---

[340] "Pretrial Justice: How Much Does It Cost?" Pretrial Justice Institute, 2017.
https://university.pretrial.org/HigherLogic/System/DownloadDocumentFile.ashx?DocumentFileKey=4c666992-0b1b-632a-13cb-b4ddc66fadcd&forceDialog=0

[341] as I previously recommended in *American Justice?*

[342] Anne Kim, "Time to Abolish Cash Bail. It doesn't keep dangerous criminals off the streets. It just keeps the poor in jail—and finance companies rolling in profits", *Washington Monthly*, January/February 2017; https://washingtonmonthly.com/magazine/januaryfebruary-2017/time-to-abolish-cash-bail

[343] ACLU Campaign for Smart Justice, "Selling off our Freedom: How insurance corporations have taken over our bail system", May 2017, p. 10.

bond, with very few of those out on bond failing to appear in court.[344]

> Utilization of computer algorithm predictions to set bail instead of relying on human judgment. A recent report suggests that machines could do better than judges, either by reducing crime 25% with no change in jailing rates or reducing jailing rates 42% with no increase in crime.[345,346]

> Increasing funding for indigent defense. Such funding would reduce the number of jailed inmates by providing them with defense lawyers less overloaded with cases.

Status of Criminal Justice Reform Efforts

Unfortunately, despite the need for criminal justice reform efforts to make changes to reduce incarcerations, recidivism, and crime, little is being accomplished at the Federal level. It is also unlikely that such reforms will be made during the current administration, since President

---

[344] "For Better of for Profit: How the Bail Bonding Industry Stands in the Way of Fair and Effective Pretrial Justice", Justice Policy Institute, September 2012; http://www.justicepolicy.org/uploads/justicepolicy/documents/_for_better_or_for_profit_.pdf

[345] Jon Kleinberg, Himabindu Lakkaraju, Jure Leskovec, Jens Ludwig and Sendhil Mullainathan, "Human Decisions and Machine Predictions", Quarterly Journal of Economics qjx032, 8/26/2017; https://doi.org/10.1093/qje/qjx0332

[346] "Machine Learning. Jail or Bail? Machines versus Judges", *Science* 358, 760, 11/10/2017.

Trump and Attorney General Sessions appear intent to pursue a more law and order approach.

By contrast, some of these reforms efforts are taking place at the state level. So far, a number of states are acting to reduce their incarceration burden and reduce corrections spending. As an example, in 2015, 30 or more states enacted changes in procedures or policy likely to reduce the numbers of incarcerated.[347] One of these states, Mississippi, managed to reduce its prison population by 15% in 2014.[348]

Ironically, some of the best suggestions for how to reform the system have come from those who have been incarcerated. It might initially be galling to consider such suggestions made by a white ex-convict who was a member of the Symbionese Liberation Army (SLA). The SLA came to prominence when wealthy heiress Patty Hearst was kidnapped and became an advocate for the cause, until she was rescued and later claimed she had been brainwashed by the group. However, I have drawn on some recommendations of James Kilgore, since they seem quite instructive and applicable to ways to improve the criminal justice system today.

---

[347] Nicole D. Porter, "The State of Sentencing 2015. Developments in Policy and Practice", The Sentencing Project, 2016; http://sentencingproject.org/wp-content/uploads/2016/02/State-of-Sentencing-2015.pdf

[348] Colleen Curry, "How Mississippi Slashed Its Prison Population and Embraced Criminal Justice Reform", *Vice News*, 9/23/2015; https://news.vice.com/article/how-mississippi-slashed-its-prison-population-and-embraced-criminal-justice-reform

Measures to Reduce Admissions

Actions to Take at the Initial Point of Contact with the System

> Institute restorative practices involving restitution to solve low-level conflict.

> Issue citations instead of arrests for minor cases.

> Offer diversion programs such as mental health courts and drug courts instead of incarceration.

> Eliminate or reduce parole or probation violations, especially technical violations.

> Reduce or eliminate arrests and criminal justice-linked processes in schools.

> Reduce bail amounts and increasingly use release without bail.

> Reduce the use of detention in immigration cases.

Long-Term Prevention/Community Development Strategies

> Inject resources into communities which have been critically affected by mass incarceration to provide for more education, job creation and training, psychological support services, substance abuse treatment, mental health facilities, and public housing.

- ➤ Increase the levels of welfare provided for various social support programs, such as Temporary Assistance for Needy Families (TANF), Supplemental Nutritional Assistance Program (SNAP), and unemployment benefits.

- ➤ Increase education and job training for people in prison.

- ➤ Retrain police so they have more racial/ethnic/gender sensitivity and better understand use of force guidelines, restorative practices, and when to call for mental health crisis intervention.

- ➤ Demilitarize the police, so they are less likely to use force in dealing with situations that call for skills in negotiation, listening, and counseling; and they use military tactics only when completely necessary.

- ➤ Increase police accountability by using video cams during citizen-police encounters over criminal activity and recording or videotaping any interviews or interrogations.

- ➤ Increase the resources paid to public defenders, including providing them with a budget to help low-income defendants charged with less serious non-violent offenses obtain bail.

Legislative Changes

- ➤ Legalize or decriminalize drug possession.

- Eliminate harsh local government ordinances aimed at survival activities such as sleeping in public and begging.

- Reduce or eliminate charges for everyday practices that are still on the books as infractions, such as jaywalking.

- Reduce or eliminate criminal justice fines as a source of income for the government.

- Reform immigration law to prevent police officers from asking for immigration papers for routine contacts with the law or for minor infractions and misdemeanors.

- Reduce barriers to employment and to benefits for people with felony convictions by dropping certain less serious crimes from public records, while leaving them available for law enforcement and court records.

- Increase the access to health care for the poor by providing them with vouchers or low cost treatment centers.

- Shorten or eliminate the terms of parole.

- Reduce financial penalties, such as payments for fines and restitution associated with criminal justice involvement, for low income defendants.

- Modify conspiracy laws, so just associating with someone involved in a crime isn't grounds for being charged with conspiracy; an individual must intentionally do something in furtherance of the criminal scheme.

➢ Revoke asset forfeiture laws.

➢ Cut back on providing military hardware to the police.

➢ Eliminate the legal penalties for truancy and other school-related "misbehavior;" let the schools handle these matters through their own disciplinary procedures.

Measures to Increase Releases

Prison/jail/court practices and policies

➢ Increase the use of non-bond pretrial release.

➢ Create incentives for early release, such as by allowing offers of employment to qualify the prisoner for early release.

➢ Increase the use of community corrections programs, such as work release and work furlough.

➢ Change sentencing practices to reduce their length, and increase time off for good behavior.

➢ Increase the opportunities for granting of good time to prisoners, or increase the amount of good time that prisoners can accumulate through good behavior or taking on additional job responsibilities while in prison. Reward prisoners for good time by a reduction in prison stays.

➤ Retrain court and prison officials so they are more sensitive to prisoners from different racial, ethnic, and gender backgrounds.

➤ Cap the number in prison and jail, and release people when the cap is exceeded; release the prisoners with the least serious offenses and most good time first.

➤ Develop a point scoring system to use in determining good behavior and making release decisions, such as offering points not only for good behavior but for special achievements and contributions made while in prison. These achievements and contributions might include getting a GED, donating blood, and taking care of the prison garden.

Legislative changes

➤ Reduce or eliminate harsh sentencing policies, such as mandatory minimums, three strikes laws, and truth in sentencing, while insisting that at least 80% of a sentence be served.

➤ Moderate sentencing guidelines or allow greater judicial flexibility in their application.

➤ Make electronic monitoring the legal equivalent of incarceration for prisoners involved in less serious and non-violent crimes.

➢ Increase the compassionate release of elderly, disabled, or extremely ill prisoners.

➢ Give prisoners time off for family responsibility, such as a serious illness or death of a family member or difficulties in dealing with a problem child.

➢ Mandate the release of prisoners serving time for the possession or sale of small amounts of drugs, especially in states where the drugs are now considered legal.

➢ Reduce or stop the allocation of funds for building prisons, jails, and other correctional facilities, and redirect the funds saved to urban communities most impacted by mass incarceration.[349]

Conclusions

There are many things we can and need to do to improve the prison system in order to both improve the lives of the incarcerated and save money at a time when budgets for public services are going down. Now that Republicans are in charge of all three branches of government, budget cuts are likely to make alternatives to incarceration even more necessary. In particular, some of the measures to reduce incarceration and cut costs that should be considered include the following:

---

[349] James Kilgore, *Understanding Mass Incarceration: A People's Guide to the Key Civil Rights Struggle of Our Time*, The New Press, 2015, p. 221.

Initially:

> Reduce recidivism by no longer sending technical violators of parole back to prison.[350]

> Stop sentencing minor drug violation offenders to prison.

> Release more prisoners who are incarcerated for minor crimes and are at the lowest risk for recidivism.

Requiring More Time to Implement:

> Reduce mandatory minimum sentencing guidelines in order to decrease the length of sentences.

> Provide greater funds for indigent defense.

> Transfer financial accountability for imprisonment from the states to the counties in order to have the counties hold the prosecutors they pay accountable for any over-incarceration they generate. If counties have to pay the price for any over-incarceration caused by their prosecutors, they won't let their prosecutors imprison so many.

> Set up sentencing commissions in each state nationwide to better assess sentencing guidelines and

---

[350] as discussed in Chapter 4.

reduce unnecessary incarcerations for less serious crimes.

➤ Establish mandatory treatment centers for prisoners with substance abuse problems instead of housing them in prison. Require such convicts to participate in these treatment programs, monitor compliance, and provide appropriate penalties for those who don't comply, including a return to prison.

➤ Reform the bail bond system to eliminate or reduce the costs for defendants so they don't spend time in jail because they can't afford a bond.

Requiring Still More Time to Implement:

➤ Introduce private prison contracts which pay for prisoner reentry results rather than for prisoner stays.

➤ Populate mental hospitals and psych wards with properly trained staff, so mentally ill prisoners can be sent there as an alternative to jail and prison.

➤ Appoint prosecutors instead of electing them, so they will not be swayed in doing their job by political or public opinion considerations.

➤ Have different prosecutors and courts for urban and suburban areas.

➢ Adopt sentencing and plea bargain guidelines to reduce sentences for less serious non-violent crimes in order to reduce or eliminate unnecessary incarcerations.

APPENDIX I

A Short Primer on Correlation Analysis

Correlation analysis is basically a simple method to determine whether two different measures may be associated with one another. It plots one measure on the X (bottom) axis and the other on the Y (left vertical) axis. It then calculates statistics to determine how likely the two parameters are associated and generates two values (r and p) to help in that determination.

The r factor can fall anywhere between 1 and -1. If the data fall on a straight line, regardless of the slope of that line, the correlation would be perfect. That would be reflected in an r factor equal to 1.0 or very close to it if the line goes up and to the right. This is shown in the first two examples below.

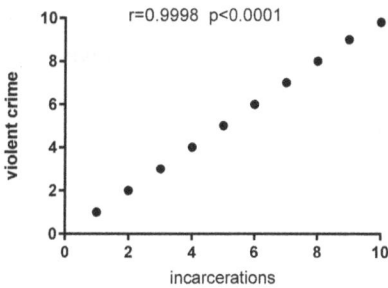

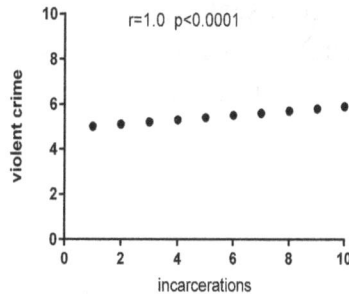

A p value is used to determine statistical significance. A p value of data that fall on a straight line would be reflected in a $p<0.0001$ (very small). Anything less than $p<0.05$ is considered statistically significant. Both plots show such small p values and therefore those correlations are statistically significant.

If, on the other hand, the line goes down and to the right, it would indicate a perfect negative correlation, reflected in an r value very close to -1. This is shown in the next plot. The very low p value again indicates high statistical significance.

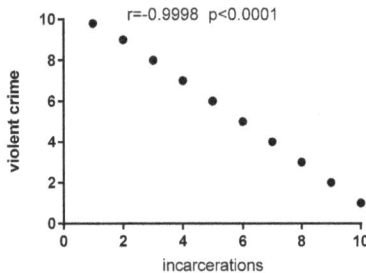

Now let's consider data that are more realistic. The more the data points fall away from a straight line or show apparent scatter, the lower the r value (for correlation) and the higher the p value (for significance). Examples of these are shown on the next page.

Below to the left is what would be considered a strong correlation (r>0.7). A trend can clearly be seen of an upward line to the right, but with more scatter than in any of the first three plots.

To the right is shown what would be considered a moderate correlation (r>0.5). You can still tell there is an upward tendency to the right, but the points are still more scattered.

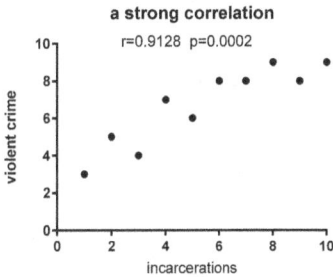

a strong correlation
r=0.9128 p=0.0002

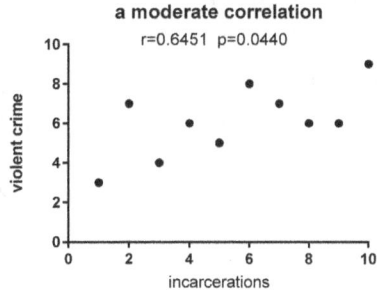

a moderate correlation
r=0.6451 p=0.0440

Note that the p values for the last two plots are larger, p=0.0002 for the strong correlation, but p=0.0440 for the moderate correlation.

When the p value is larger than 0.05, the correlation is considered not significant, regardless of the r value.

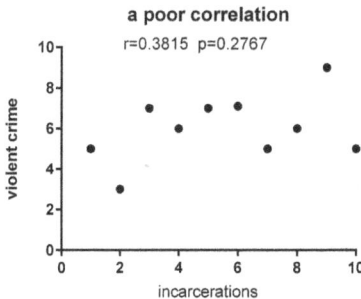

a poor correlation
r=0.3815 p=0.2767

An example of that is shown for a poor correlation on the previous page. Here, even though the r value is above that which would normally be considered a weak correlation (r>0.3), the high p value (0.2767) renders the correlation not significant and therefore poor.

In all these cases, it is important to note that even a strong correlation is insufficient to conclude that increases in one parameter (e.g., incarceration) cause increases in the other parameter (e.g., violent crime) or vice versa, although both might be considered possible. This is because changes in a third, unplotted parameter might be responsible for increases in both the parameters plotted.

APPENDIX II

Other Authors' Conclusions Regarding the Causes of the Decline in Crime

My own analysis, that 1993-2005 was when incarceration had its greatest effect (pp. 27-28), differs somewhat from the impression some liberals have put forth, that the 1980s were a time when incarceration had its greatest effect. For instance, Berkeley liberals estimated that when crime was high and incarceration relatively low in the 1980s, locking up one person in prison for one year prevented 2.5 violent crimes and 11.4 property crimes.[351] However, that success rate in preventing crimes by incarcerating a criminal fell to 0.3 violent crimes and 2.7 property crimes in the 1990s, and similar effects on crime might have been reached without resorting to imprisonment. Although our analyses differ with respect to when incarceration had its greatest effect,[352] both sets of analyses suggest incarceration did little to decrease crime after 2005.

---

[351] Rucker Johnson and Steven Raphael "How Much Crime Reduction Does the Marginal Prisoner Buy?," *Journal of Law and Economics*, 55, 275-310, 2012.

[352] My conclusion differs from that of Johnson and Raphael, who concluded that incarceration was having a reduced effect on crime in the 1990s. I believe that the problem lies in their overly complex model and their pooling data into only two groups - one during the 1978-1990 rise in incarceration and a second group of similarly pooled data from 1991 to 2004 -- and then comparing them. Thus, even though Johnson and Raphael concluded that incarceration was less effective at reducing violent and property crimes in the 1990s, this is precisely when I conclude that incarceration was the most effective against violent crime. A possible reconciliation of the conclusions of my study and theirs might

Zimring, another Berkeley author, has analyzed the decline in crime somewhat differently.[353] He downplays the role of incarceration alone by stating that it should have caused decreases in crime much earlier. He concludes that many of the other proposed causes for the nationwide decline in violent crime can be ruled out. For instance, he rules out enhanced abortions and more policing by noting that Canada had a similar decline in crime without having an increase in the number of abortions or more police. He believes that most of the crime decrease is due to a reduction in the number young (18-24 year old) individuals at highest risk for committing crimes, coupled with increased incarceration and improvements in the economy. He does not believe that more policing was responsible, except for the more rapid decline in crime in New York City. Still, other factors might have contributed, such as having more police officers, more stop-and-frisk stops, and more efficient COMPSTAT[354] tactics.

Another researcher, Peter M. Enns concluded from his analysis that the crime rate influenced public punitiveness, which in turn drove increased incarceration. However, he concluded that only 2-33% of the subsequent reduction in crime was due to increased incarceration. He came to this conclusion after analyzing data in which he found a weak correlation ($r=0.31$) with respect to the crime rate and incarceration rate over the whole period between 1950 and

---

be that a certain level of incarceration had to be present before additional ones could actually begin to demonstrate a downtick in crime.
[353] Franklin E. Zimring, *The Great American Crime Decline*, Oxford University Press, 2007.
[354] COMPSTAT refers to a form of intense monitoring of crime within different precincts by placing more officers in locations of high crime and assessing the results.

2010.[355] However, when he correlated the crime rate and the annual change in incarceration rate, he observed a much stronger correlation (r=0.72).[356] Thus, he concluded that public punitiveness and the change in incarceration rate are even more highly correlated (r=0.82).

What caused the decline in crime? Was the increased incarceration responsible or something else? Steven Levitt[357] concluded that the following factors were not materially important for the decline in crime in the 1990s:

- lower unemployment due to a strong economy,
- an aging population or other changing demographics,
- better policing strategies like community policing and identifying crime hot spots,
- gun control laws,
- laws permitting carrying of concealed weapons, or
- more death penalty executions.

Rather, he suggested the following were more substantive contributors to the reduction in violent crime:

1) increased incarceration,
2) legalized abortion (!!),[358]
3) increased numbers of police, and
4) the decline of the crack cocaine epidemic, in that order.

---

[355] Peter K. Enns, *Incarceration Nation: How the United States Became the Most Punitive Democracy in the World*, Cambridge University Press, 2016, pp. 103-9.

[356] In Appendix III, I discuss the relative merits of correlating violent crime with incarcerations or annual changes in incarceration.

[357] Steven D. Levitt, "Understanding Why Crime Fell in the 1990s: Four Factors That Explain The Decline and Six That Do Not," *Journal of Economic Perspectives*, volume 18,163-190, 2004.

[358] Supposedly because unwanted children were more likely to grow up to be criminals.

While increased incarceration and increased police may well have played roles in decreasing crime rates, the abortion argument is ridiculous and totally unacceptable to conservatives. While crack may have had an impact previously, it has had little impact lately, and therefore offers no clue for seriously reducing crime further today.[359] Levitt was puzzled that his prognostications had also predicted a crime decline from 1973 to 1991 which had not occurred. This indicates that something must have been incorrect about some of his analysis.

A contributor to the increased incarceration that reduced violent crime is likely to have been longer sentences. In *Why Are So Many Americans in Prison?*,[360] Raphael and Stoll concluded that longer sentences contributed more to the growing prison population than increased prison admissions.

---

[359] However, the contribution of our current opioid epidemic might represent its more recent counterpart.

[360] Steven Raphael and Michael A. Stoll, *Why Are So Many Americans in Prison?*, Russell Sage Foundation, 2013.

APPENDIX III

Comparisons Between Correlations of Incarcerations vs. Changes in Incarcerations

The correlation below plots total incarcerations in a given year against violent crime, and it is weak because there appear to be three or four different phases to it, each of which would likely yield much stronger correlations.

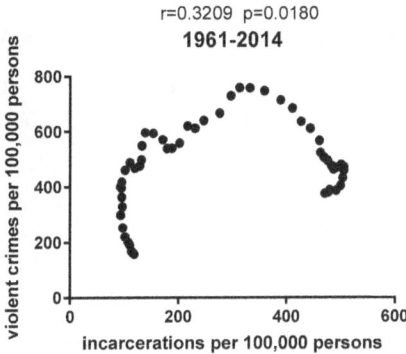

r=0.3209 p=0.0180
1961-2014

violent crimes per 100,000 persons
incarcerations per 100,000 persons

A much stronger correlation is obtained with respect to the annual change in incarceration:

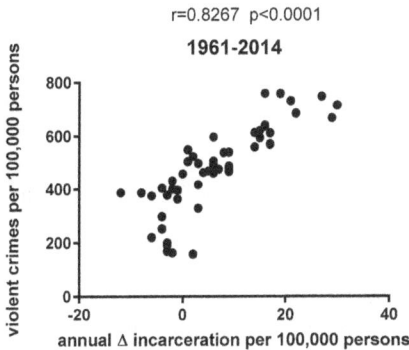

r=0.8267 p<0.0001
1961-2014

violent crimes per 100,000 persons
annual Δ incarceration per 100,000 persons

In this case, the x axis plots the change (Δ) in incarcerations from year to year, and a much stronger correlation is obtained (0.8267 vs. 0.3209) with better statistical significance (<0.0001 vs. 0.0180).

However, in both correlations, data from all years are grouped together. A very different result is obtained if one looks at incarcerations per 100,000 persons (100K) vs. the annual change (Δ) during the different legs of the curve shown in the first graph above. This is shown in the following table:

THE RELATIONSHIP BETWEEN INCARCERATION AND VIOLENT CRIME FROM 1961 TO 2014.

	r value[361]		p value[362]	
years	Incarcerations per 100K	Annual Δ	Incarcerations per 100K	Annual Δ
1961-1973	0.8884	0.3688	<0.0001	0.2150
1974-1992	0.9392	0.7048	<0.0001	<0.0001
1993-2005	**-0.9791**	0.9387	<0.0001	<0.0001
2006-2014	0.829	0.8705	0.0057	0.0023

---

[361] The r value indicates how little scatter (deviation from a straight line) there is to the correlation.

[362] The p value indicates the statistical significance of the correlation. The lower the number, the greater the statistical significance. Any number over 0.05 is not considered statistically significant.

Several features of this table should be noted. Only the incarceration rate correlation for 1993-2005 exhibits a negative correlation. That is not seen in the annual change correlation, which suggests that the annual change correlation completely misses a significant finding. Second, in the four different legs of the curve, analysis involving incarcerations per 100K yields stronger correlations (3/4) with statistics as good or better than the annual change correlation.

I believe this shows that for most purposes, it is better to look at correlations over shorter periods of time than longer ones because changes in conditions might occur that affect the correlations. Correlations over a longer period of time ignore those potentially important changes.

APPENDIX IV

Minor Influences on the Simultaneous Reductions of New York City Violent Crime and Incarceration

In his book *The City that Became Safe*, Franklin
Zimring used a process of elimination to systematically rule
out a number of possible causes for the decrease in violent
crime before he settled on what he considered the principal
causes, related in Chapter 4 of this book. In this Appendix, I
summarize some of his reasoning regarding causes of no or
minor contribution to the decrease in violent crime in New
York City, and I follow up on some of these issues with some
further correlation analyses of my own.

First, Zimring ruled out the effect of a large urban
environment by showing that the 1990 to 2007 decrease in
homicide and violent crime was greater in New York City
than in other large U.S. cities, even when he broke New York
City up into its separate boroughs. He next ruled out
demographic changes in racial or ethnic composition by
comparing changes in crime rates in New York's different
boroughs. He then ruled out changes in unemployment,
youth unemployment, poverty, and the proportion of single
parent households, because all of these were greater in New
York City than in the U.S. throughout the same time period.
During this time, the proportion of 15 to 29 year olds
decreased more in New York City than in the U.S., but it did
not decrease enough to account for the crime decrease,
especially considering that the proportion of 15-19 year olds
increased and the proportion of youth failing to finish high
school remained constant. He ruled out changes in drug use,
because New York City continued to have higher rates of

cocaine and heroin use than the U.S. as a whole throughout the 1990-2007 period.[363] Until 1991, violent crime and incarceration both were increasing in New York City, and during this period, increased prison admissions and violent crime were correlated, but the relationship changed markedly after 1992, when violent crime started to be reduced (right):

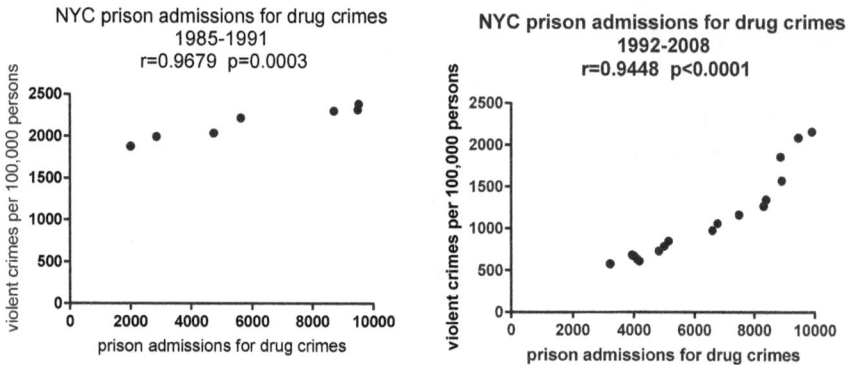

NYC prison admissions for drug crimes 1985-1991 r=0.9679 p=0.0003

NYC prison admissions for drug crimes 1992-2008 r=0.9448 p<0.0001

Since much violent crime is associated with the drug trade, it may not be so surprising that a greater than 75% reduction in one is associated with a similar reduction in the other. However, it may not be possible to determine whether it was the decrease in drug prison admissions that caused the decrease in violent crime or the other way around.

Next, I consider other drug use.

---

[363] Indeed, using data provided by Kyle T Bernstein, Angela Bucciarelli, Tinka Markham Piper, Charles Gross, Ken Tardiff and Sandro Galea, "Cocaine- and opiate-related fatal overdose in New York City, 1990-2000", BMC Public Health 7:31 doi:10.1186/1471-2458-7-31 and New York City Department of Health and Mental Hygiene, "Unintentional Drug Poisoning (Overdose) Deaths Involving Heroin and/or Fentanyl in New York City, 2000-2015", Epi Data Brief, August, 2016, No. 74, I found no correlation between fatal overdoses and either violent crime or NYC-derived incarcerations.

Misdemeanor Arrests for Marijuana

When they were relatively few, increasing misdemeanor marijuana arrests correlated well with a *decrease* in violent crime between 1978 and 1996 (left). This was a time when violent crime both rose and fell.

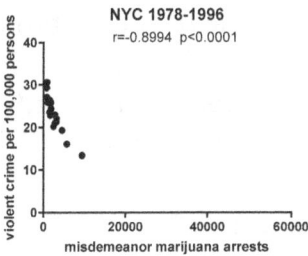

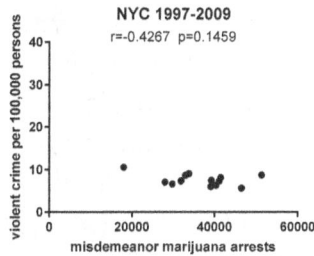

However, when misdemeanor marijuana arrests grew massively further between 1997 and 2009, the correlation was poor and not statistically significant (right). Furthermore, there was no good positive or negative correlation between misdemeanor marijuana arrests and incarceration rate for the 1997-2009 period (not shown; r=-0.3695, p=0.2140). Thus, misdemeanor marijuana arrests may have helped reduce violent crime up until the mid1990s, but still more arrests after that didn't reduce violent crime or incarceration.

The Influence of the Broken Windows and Stop and Frisk Approaches

Two policing policies were introduced by the Giuliani administration at roughly the same time.

Broken Windows

Fixing "broken windows" was a policy designed to discourage even petty crime and graffiti and thereby promote a safer environment. Mayors Giuliani and DeBlasio as well as NY police commissioners Bratton and Kelley all argued that fixing broken windows -- a term used to refer to neighborhood deterioration generally -- was primarily responsible for the decrease in NYC crime.[364]

However, it is difficult to quantitate the elements of the broken windows policy, and easier to quantitate stop-and-frisk incidents. Both policies greatly affected and angered the

---

[364] Chris Hayes, *A Colony in a Nation*, W.W. Norton, 2017, Chapter V.

black community, yet they may have contributed to small reductions in violent crime and lowered incarceration rates.

Stop-and-Frisk Policing

Stop and frisk policing ballooned over 6 times from 2002 to 2013 under Mayor Bloomberg, until it was stopped by a federal judge since more than half of those stopped were black and another 30% Hispanics. Half of the 4.4 million stop and frisk stops involved frisks for weapons, but only 1.5% of those frisks discovered weapons, and only 6% of stops resulted in arrests and another 6% in summons.[365]

The crime rate fell not only when stop-and-frisk was the NYPD policy, but also when that policy was stopped; thus

---

[365] Marc Lamont Hill, *Nobody: Casualties of America's War on the Vulnerable, Ferguson to Flint and Beyond*, 2017, p. 58.

the homicide rate was not correlated with (affected by) the incarceration rate.[366]

While stopping and frisking suspects correlated with decreased violent crime (below, left) and with decreased incarceration (below, right), it would have taken a huge number of stops to reduce violent crime or incarceration by half.

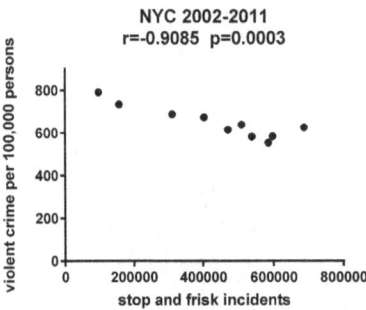

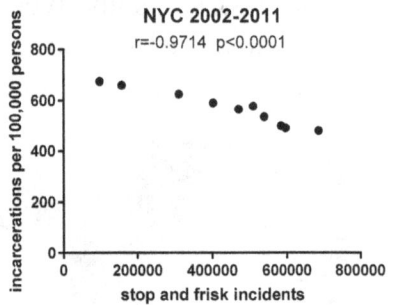

Lead Toxicity

Other factors, including a decrease in lead toxicity from paint, have been suggested to have contributed to the decrease in crime.[367] It seems like a stretch to make this connection, but perhaps a reduction in this toxicity, which contributes to mental illness, might have had an impact, since

---

[366] "Crime and Gratitude in New York," *New York Times*, January 1, 2017

[367] Jennifer L. Doleac, "New Evidence that Lead Exposure Increases Crime", Brookings Institute, 6/1/2017; https://www.brookings.edu/blog/up-front/2017/06/01/new-evidence-that-lead-exposure-increases-crime

a high percentage of the criminal population that is incarcerated suffers from a mental illness. Therefore, if you reduce the number of individuals suffering from mental illness by reducing lead toxicity from paint and leaded gasoline, maybe this could have led to a reduction in the number of criminals and therefore lower arrests and lower incarcerations. Given the high levels of lead in drinking water found recently in Flint and other cities, this possibility may deserve serious inquiry and research. After all, many water lines are still made of lead. However, given the continuously high numbers of mentally ill prisoners, lead toxicity may not have abated enough for it to be much of a contributory factor.

Summing Up

To summarize, the following factors are likely to have contributed to the reduction in violent crime:

- ❖ Increased incarceration
- ❖ Increased police on the beat
- ❖ Longer sentencing

The following probably paid a more minor role:

- ❖ Misdemeanor marijuana arrests
- ❖ Broken windows
- ❖ Stop and frisk arrests

And the following requires more scrutiny to assess:

- ❖ Decreases in lead levels leading to decreased mental illness

ABOUT THE AUTHOR

Paul Brakke is a scientist based in central Arkansas. He became interested in the criminal justice system because, as described in his first book *American Justice?,* his life was turned upside down by the system. This occurred after his wife was falsely accused of aggravated assault for trying to run over a 12-year old boy with her car. A group of kids and some neighbors wanted her out of the neighborhood. Eventually, the Brakkes were forced to move as part of a plea agreement, since otherwise, Brakke's wife was threatened with a possible 16-year jail sentence if the case went to trial and she lost.

After an initial critique of the criminal justice system, he went on to look at other problems in the system and the country in general and how to fix them. His other books now include: *The Price of Justice, Cops Aren't Such Bad Guys, The Great National Divides,* and *Fixing the U.S. Criminal Justice System.*

Now he has added this book. Over the past four years, he has become an expert on the criminal justice system and has become a speaker and consultant on this topic. He has also set up a publishing company American Leadership Books, featuring books on criminal justice and social issues which are available in print and e-books through Amazon, Ingram, Kindle, and other major distributors.

The books' websites are www.americanleadershipbooks.com and www.americanjusticethebook.com.

OTHER AVAILABLE BOOKS

American Justice?
https://www.amazon.com/American-Justice-Paul-Brakke/dp/069271068X

The Price of Justice in America
https://www.amazon.com/Price-Justice-America-Commentaries-Criminal/dp/154063289X

Cops Aren't Such Bad Guys
https://www.amazon.com/Cops-Arent-Such-Bad-Guys/dp/1542605792

The Great National Divides
https://www.amazon.com/Great-National-Divides-Divided-Together/dp/1545045631

The Great National Divides (in Full Color)
https://www.amazon.com/Great-National-Divides-Full-Color/dp/1947466038

Fixing the U.S. Criminal Justice System
https://www.amazon.com/Fixing-U-S-Criminal-Justice-System/dp/1977606989

CONTACT US

For more information:

AMERICAN LEADERSHIP BOOKS
Little Rock, Arkansas
(501) 503-8614
brakkep@gmail.com